The most terrifying fact
about the universe
is not that it is hostile,
but that it is indifferent.

CITY OF QUIET LIGHTS

Photography by Steven Shen

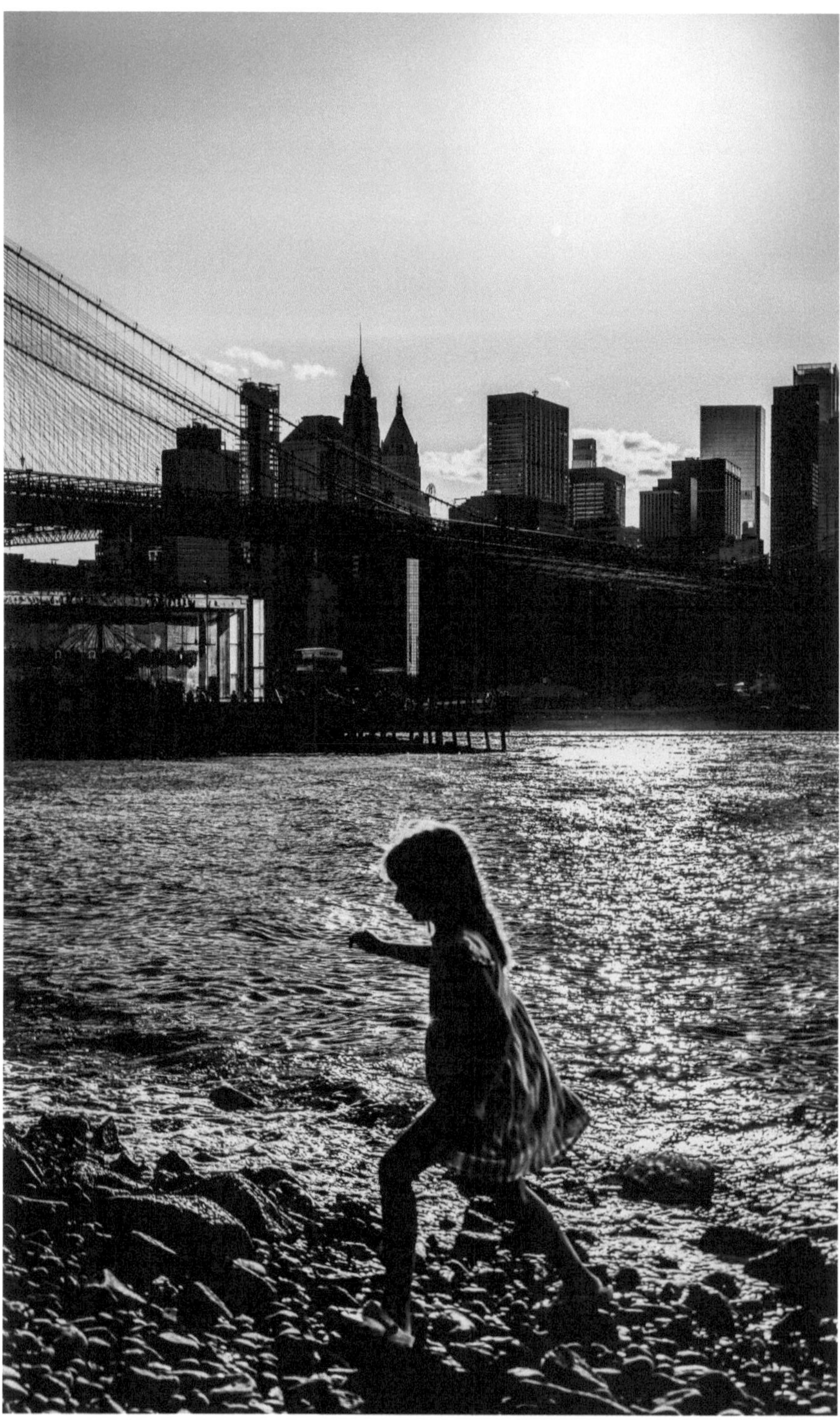

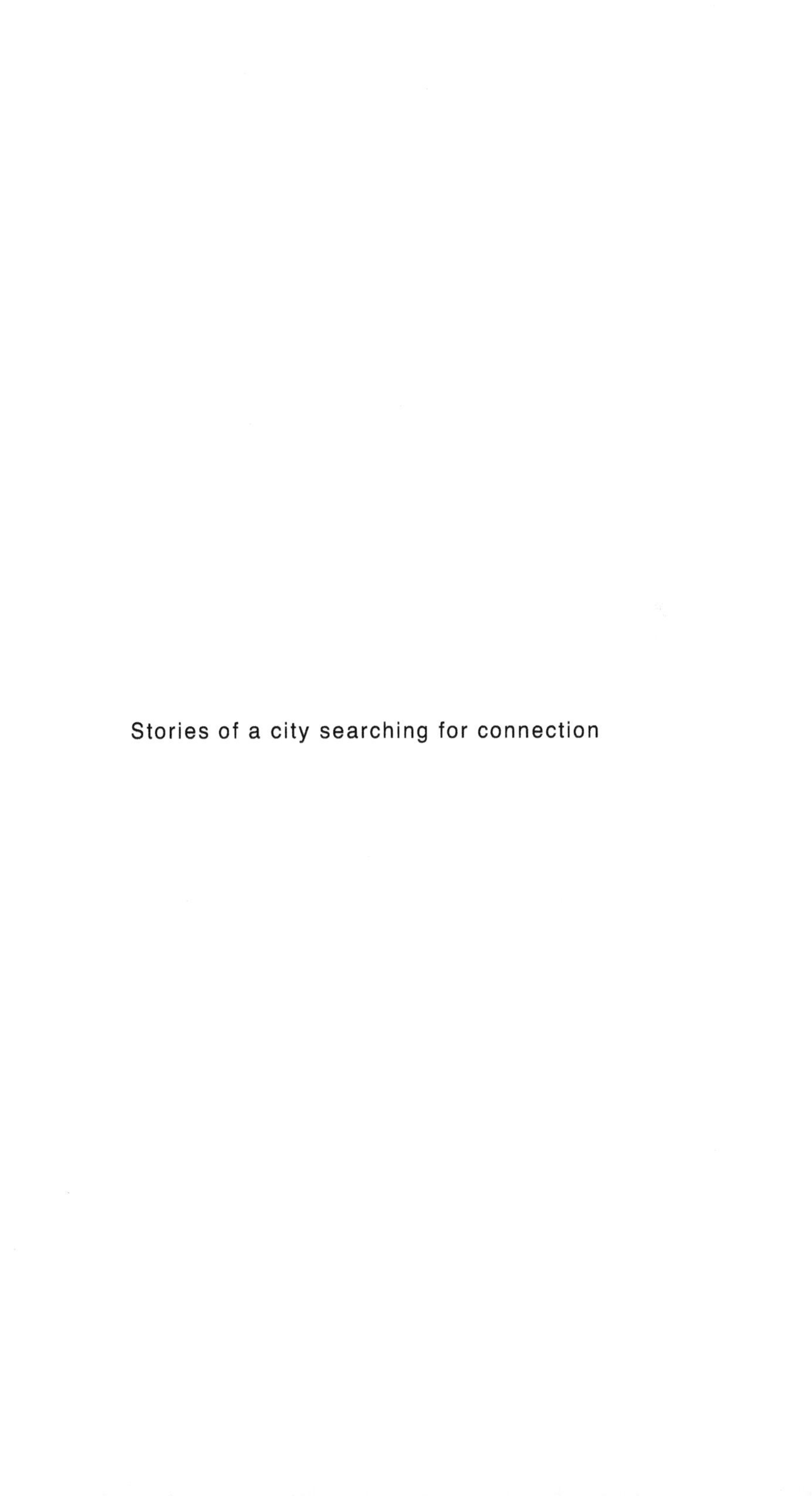

Stories of a city searching for connection

FORWARD

"He adored this City."

At the edge of a city where steel meets water light, a fleeting silhouette slips across the rocks—as if lifting the weight of New York for just one brief moment.

This photobook begins here, in a space suspended between light and shadow, between reality and longing.

New York constantly forces us to search for meaning amid its noise, and to embrace ourselves in the middle of solitude. It fascinates, and it confuses; it makes us crave understanding, even as we keep running away from one another.

These photographs are not portraits of the city's surface, but traces we leave within it: hesitation, courage, affection, anxiety, and those pockets of tenderness that ask for no witness.

If urban life is a film that never pauses, then this book is a collection of fragments I've gathered along the way— and I hope they illuminate some unnamed place in your heart.

Steven Shen
Sydney / New York
January 2026

CHAPTERS

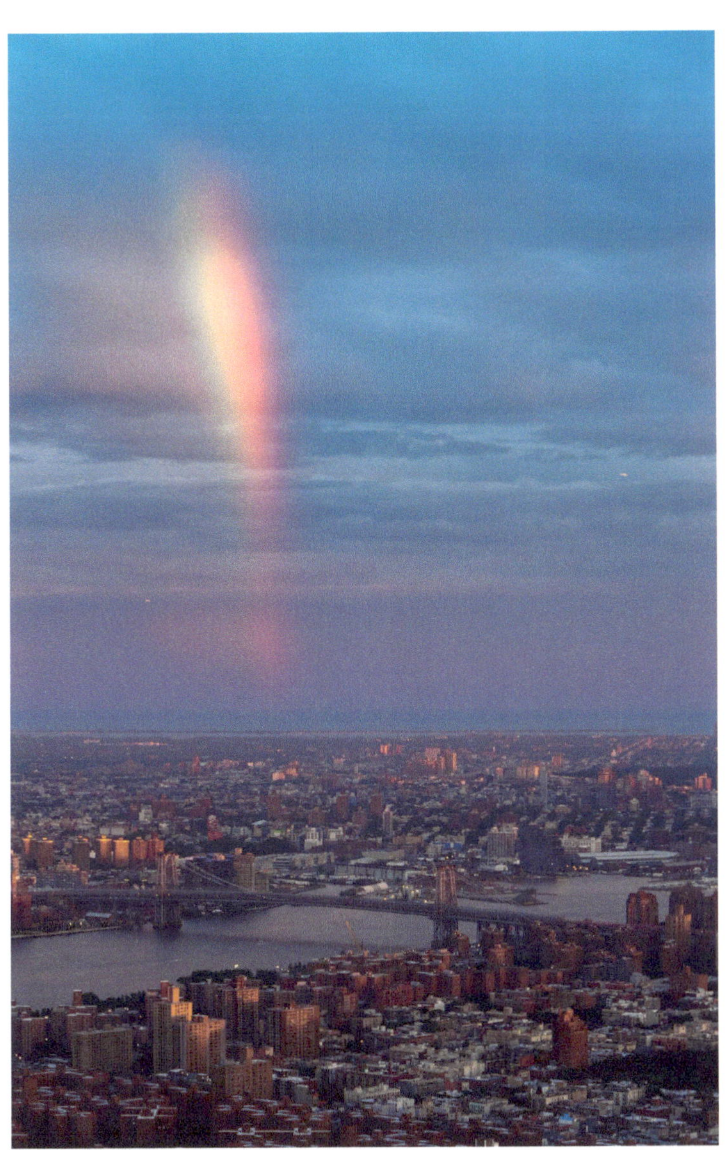

CH 1 . EDGE OF LIGHT

When light loosens its grip on darkness,
the city releases its first quiet breath.

Buildings stand like unfinished sentences,
streets trembling in the narrow seam before dawn.
Light settles into the city's metal spine,
and into parts of us not yet ready to receive it.

New York, in this chapter, has not yet shaken off its sleep.
It is about the breath we take before entering—
anticipation, hesitation, courage,
and the moment light gently urges us forward.

Edge of Light is the threshold.
Every story begins here.

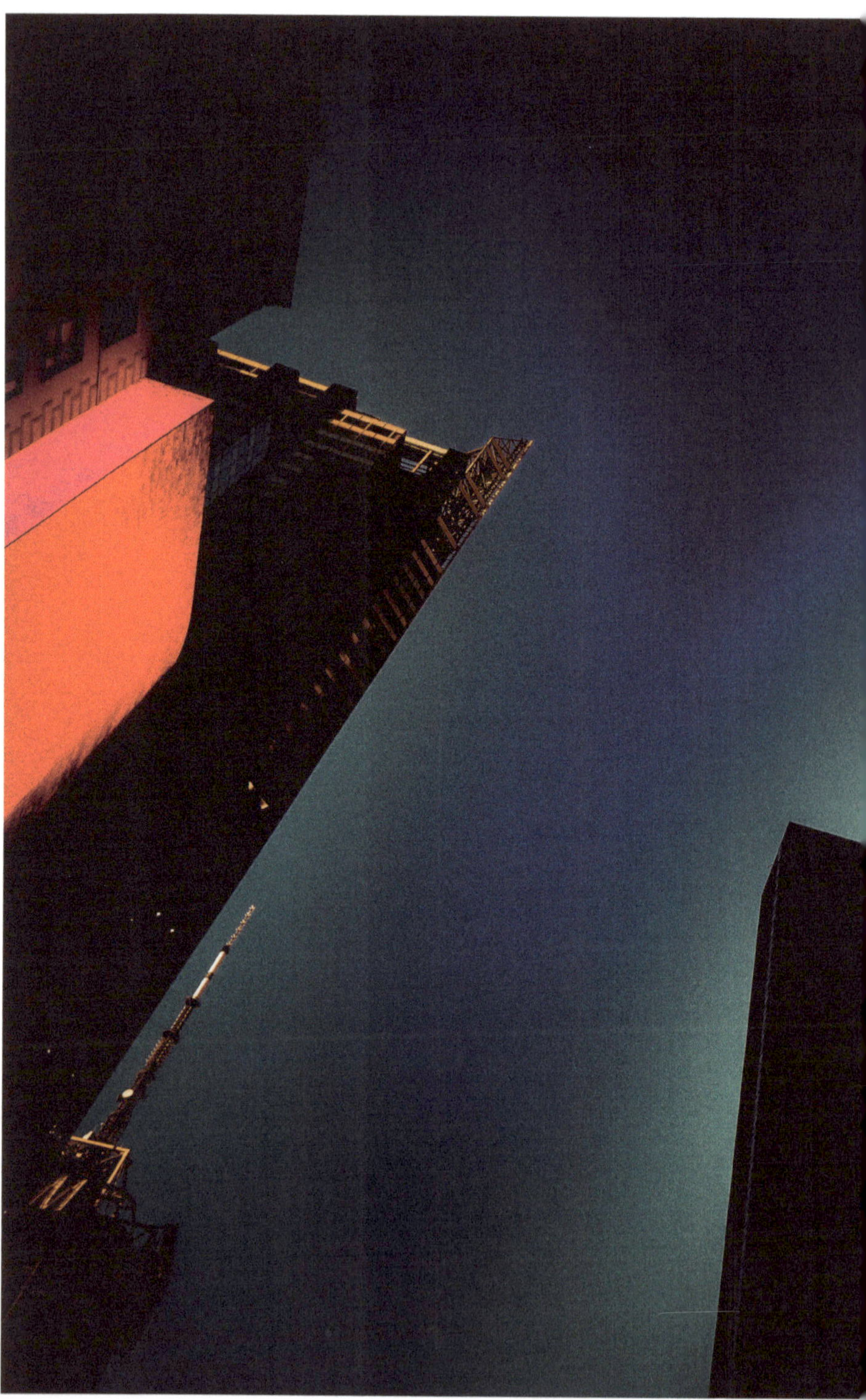

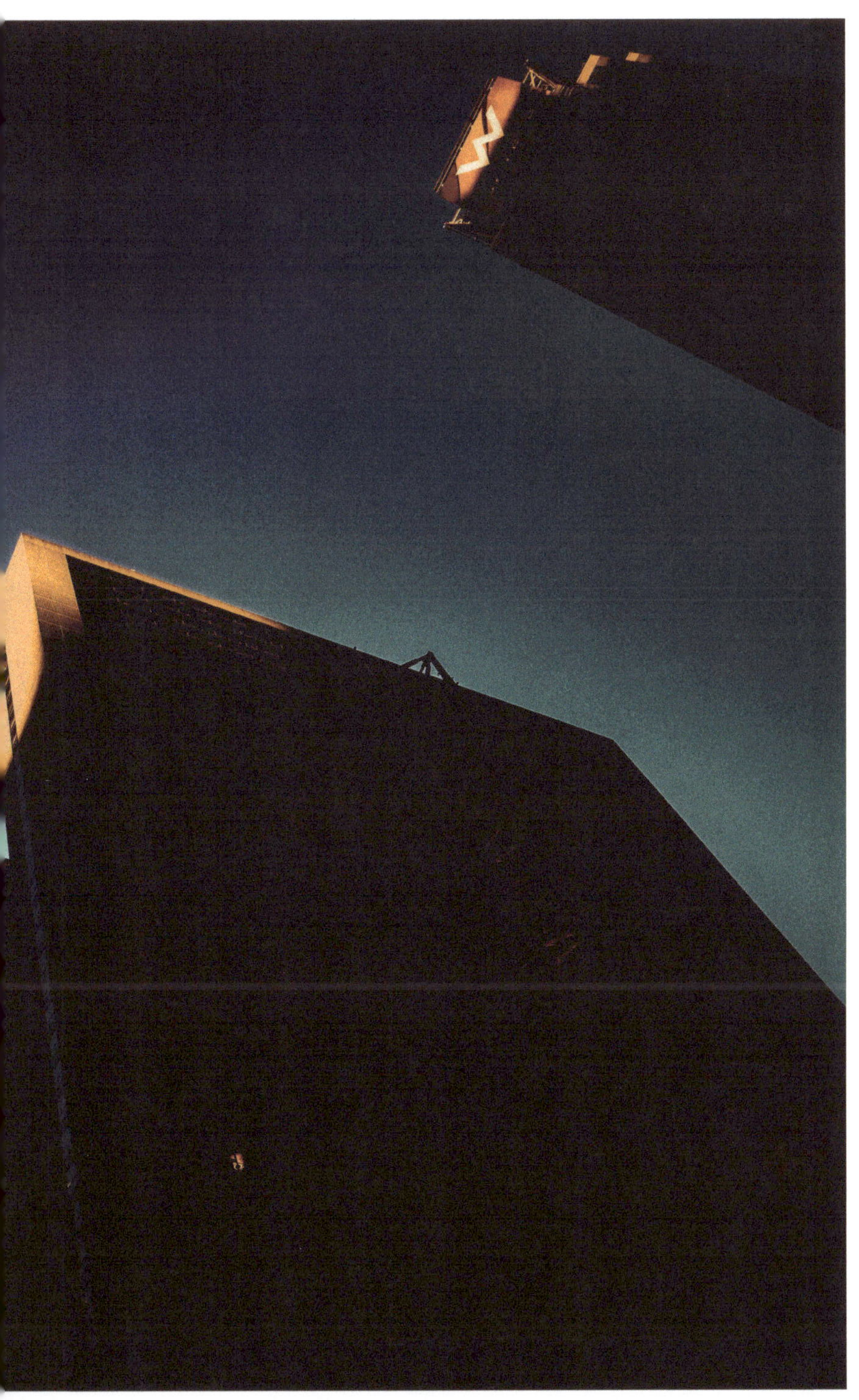

To look up is to remember you once believed in impossible things.

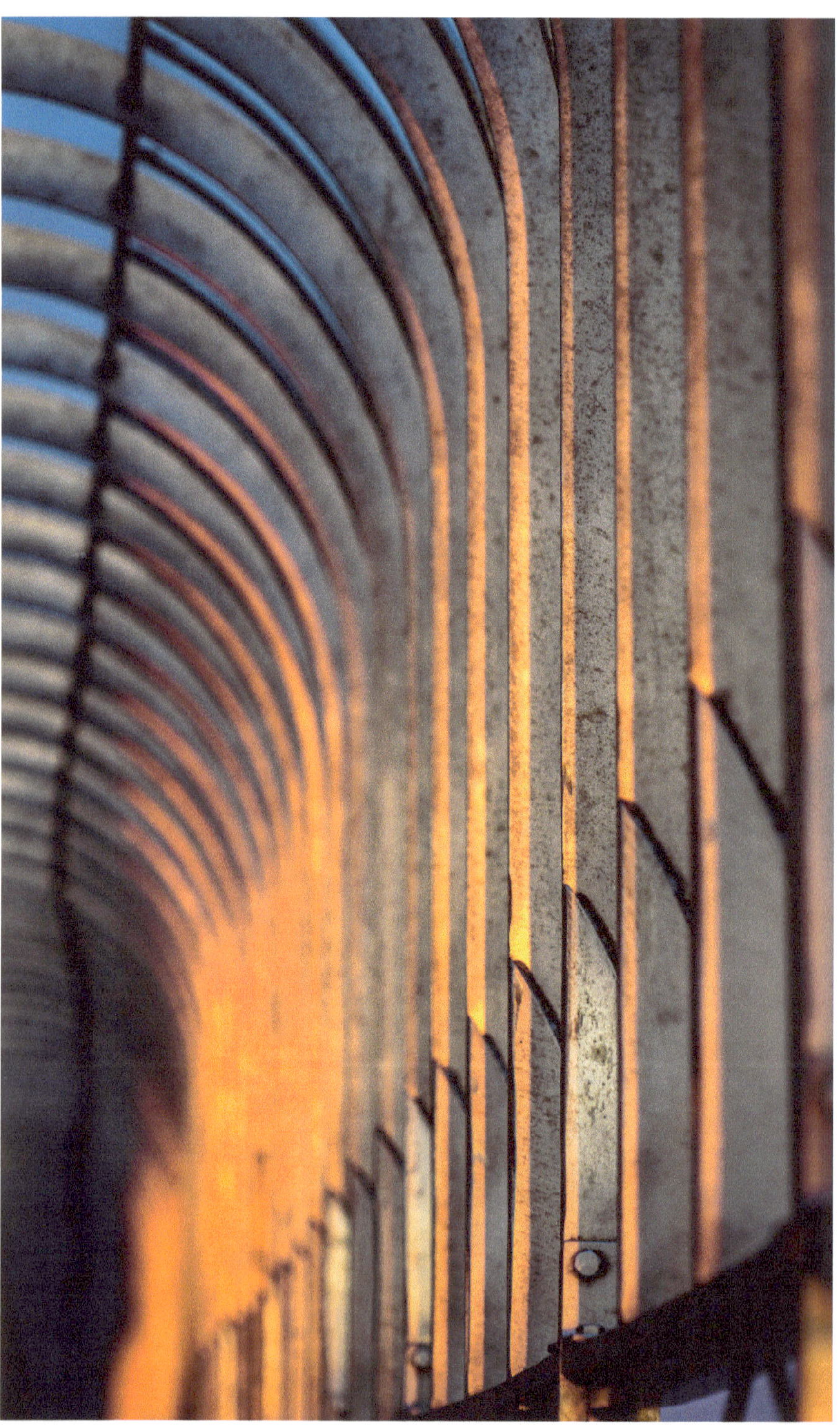

Light bends, and with it, the stories we try to hide.

The city calls your name long before you're ready to answer.

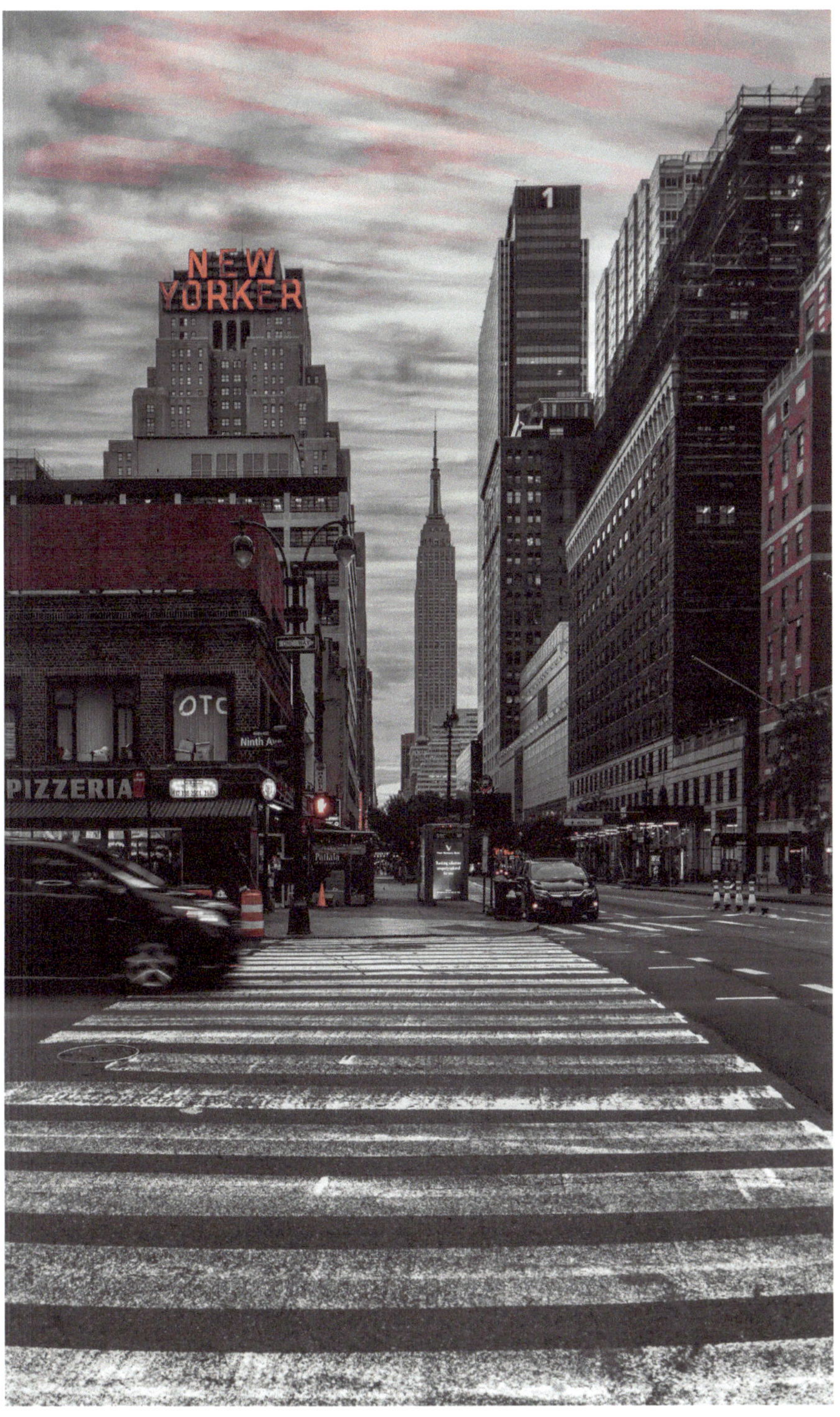

12

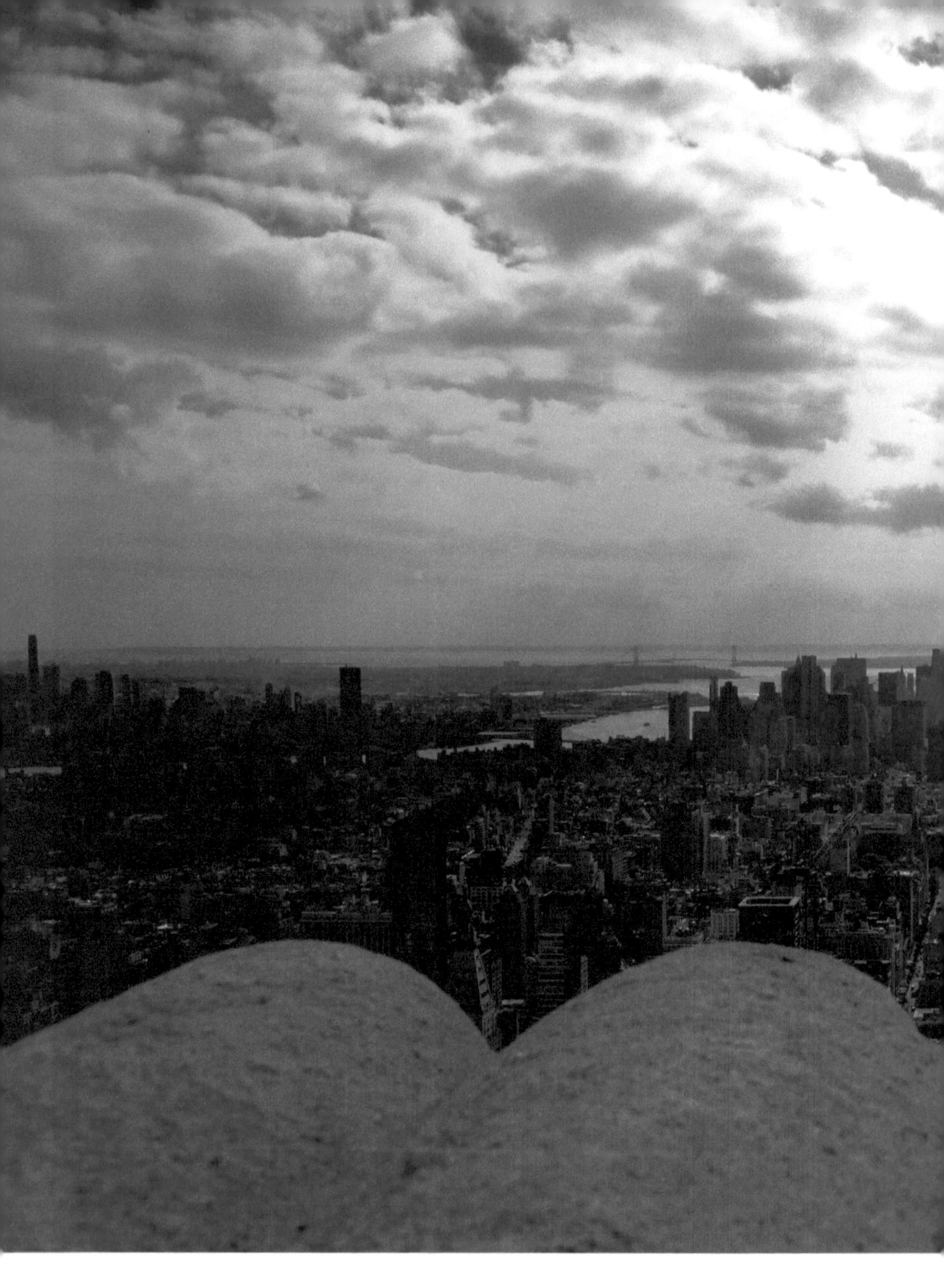

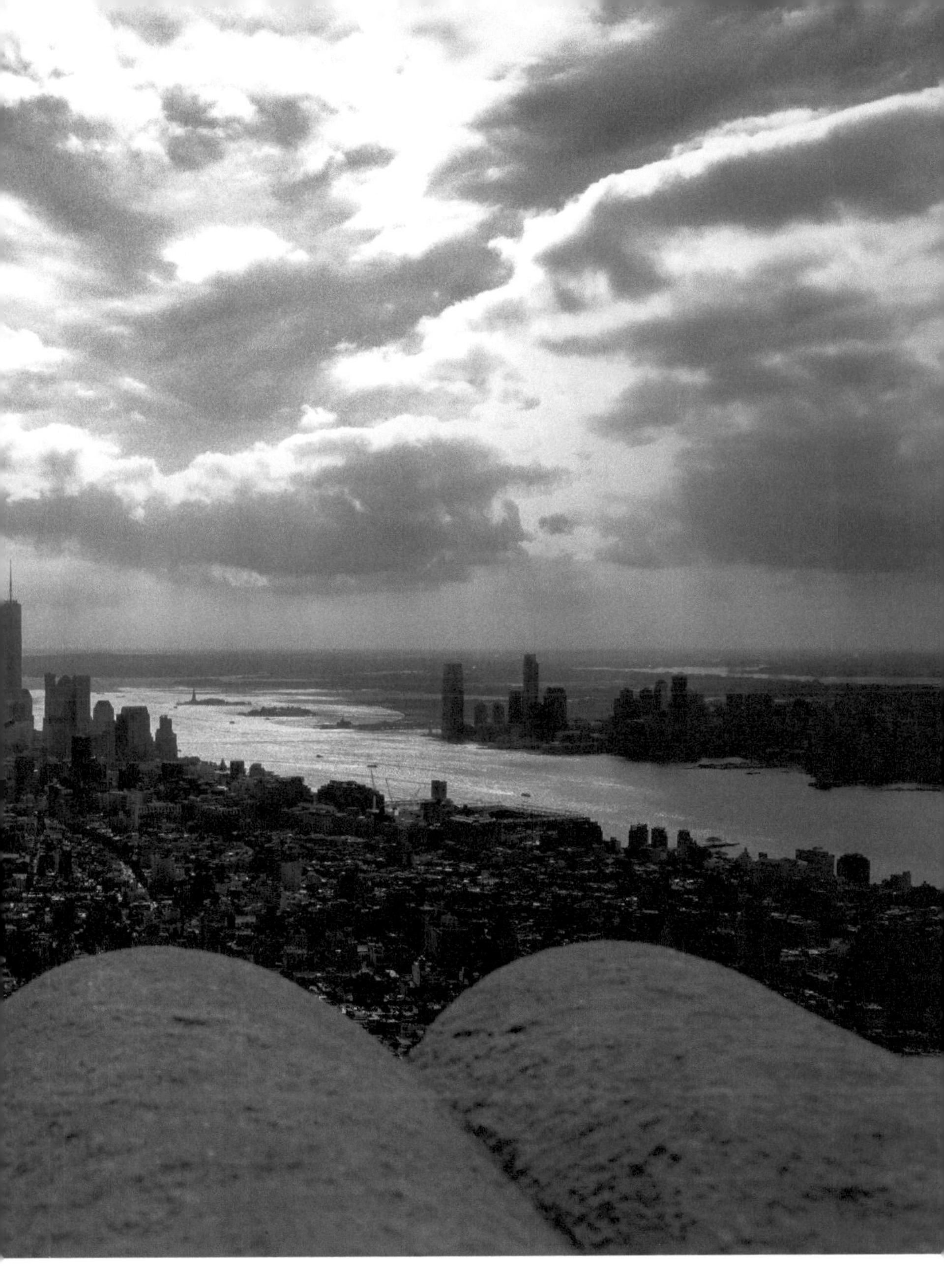

From a distance, the city breathes before it speaks.

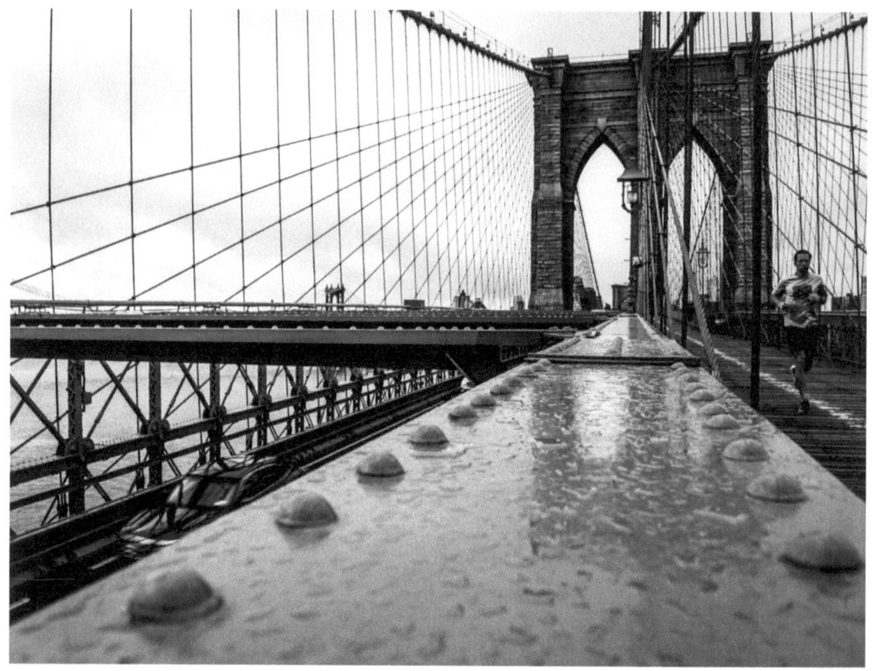

He is trying to catch the day before it fully begins.

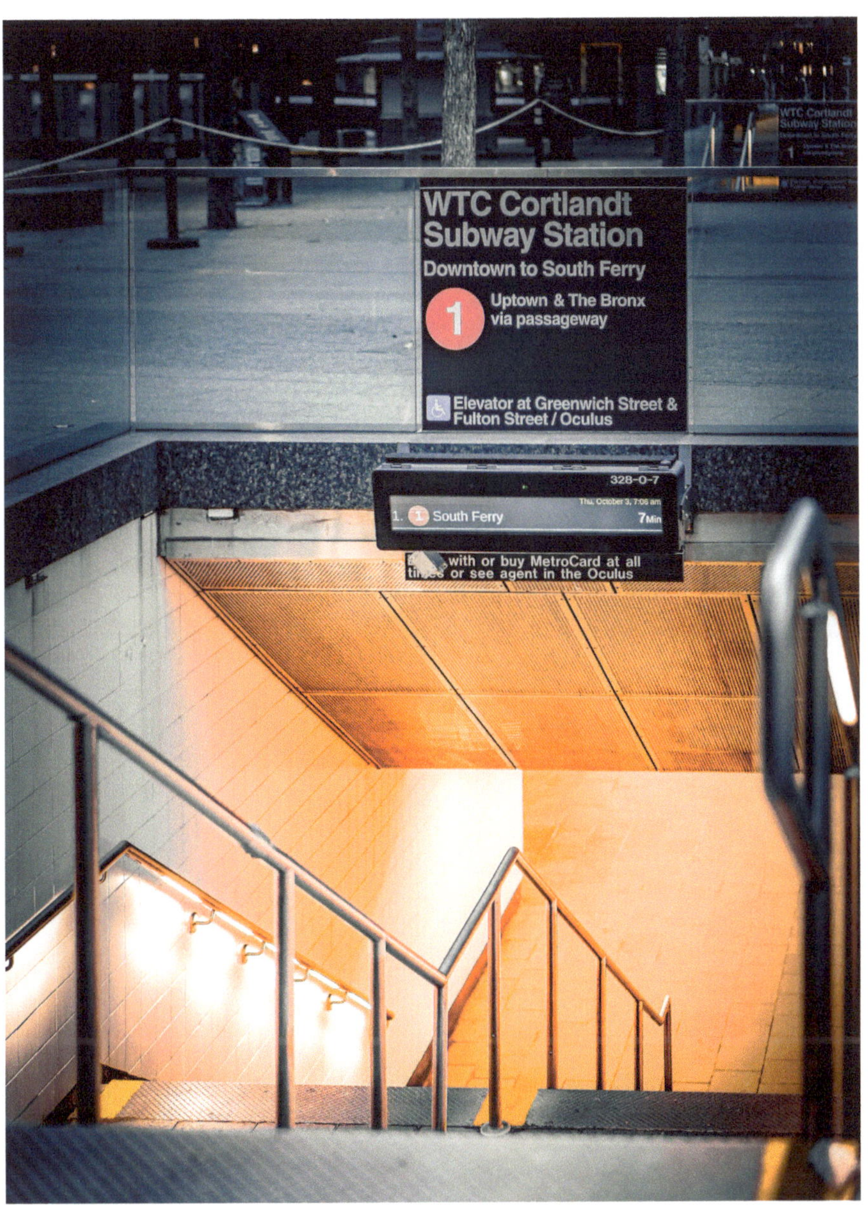

Some descents feel like beginnings.

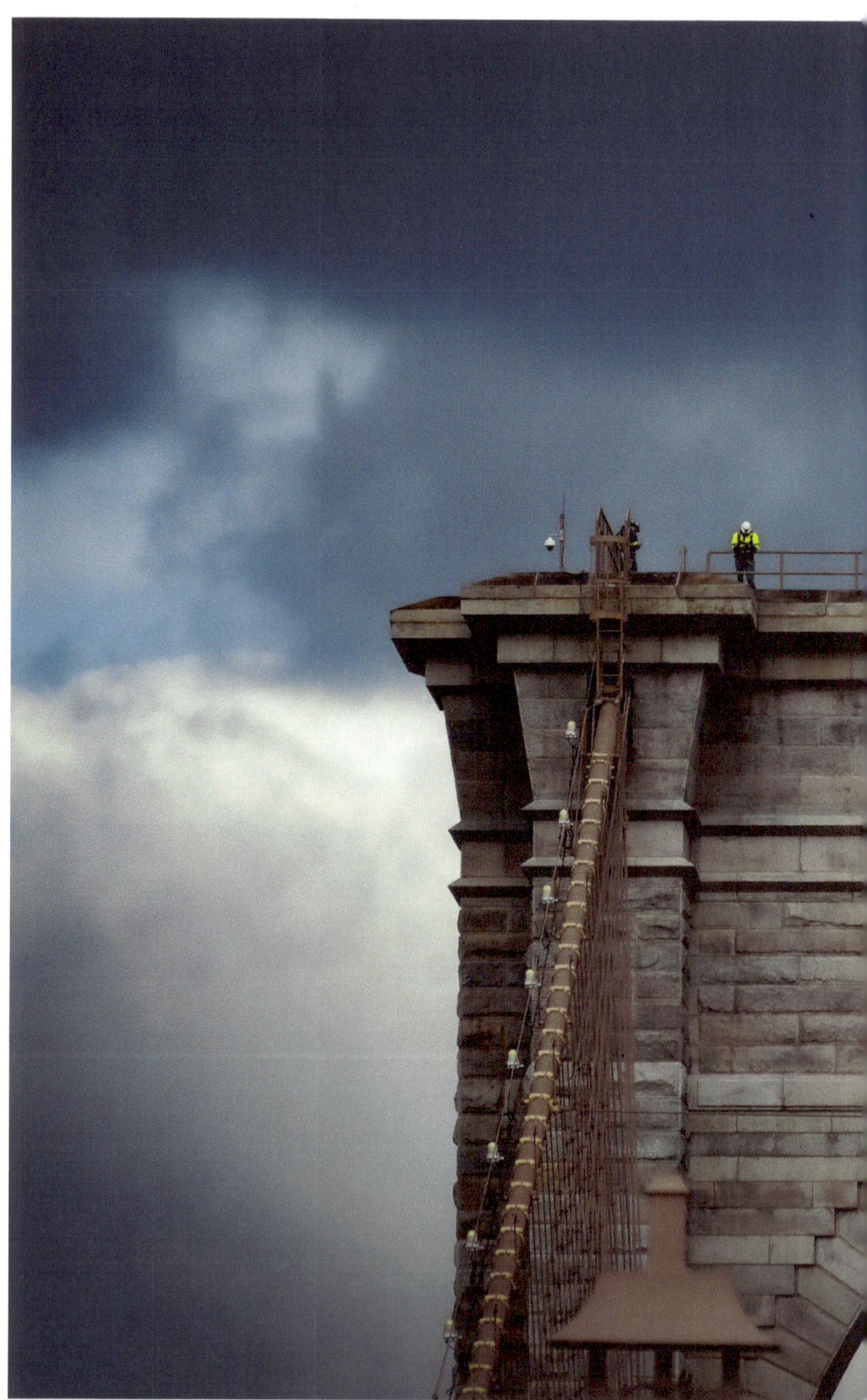

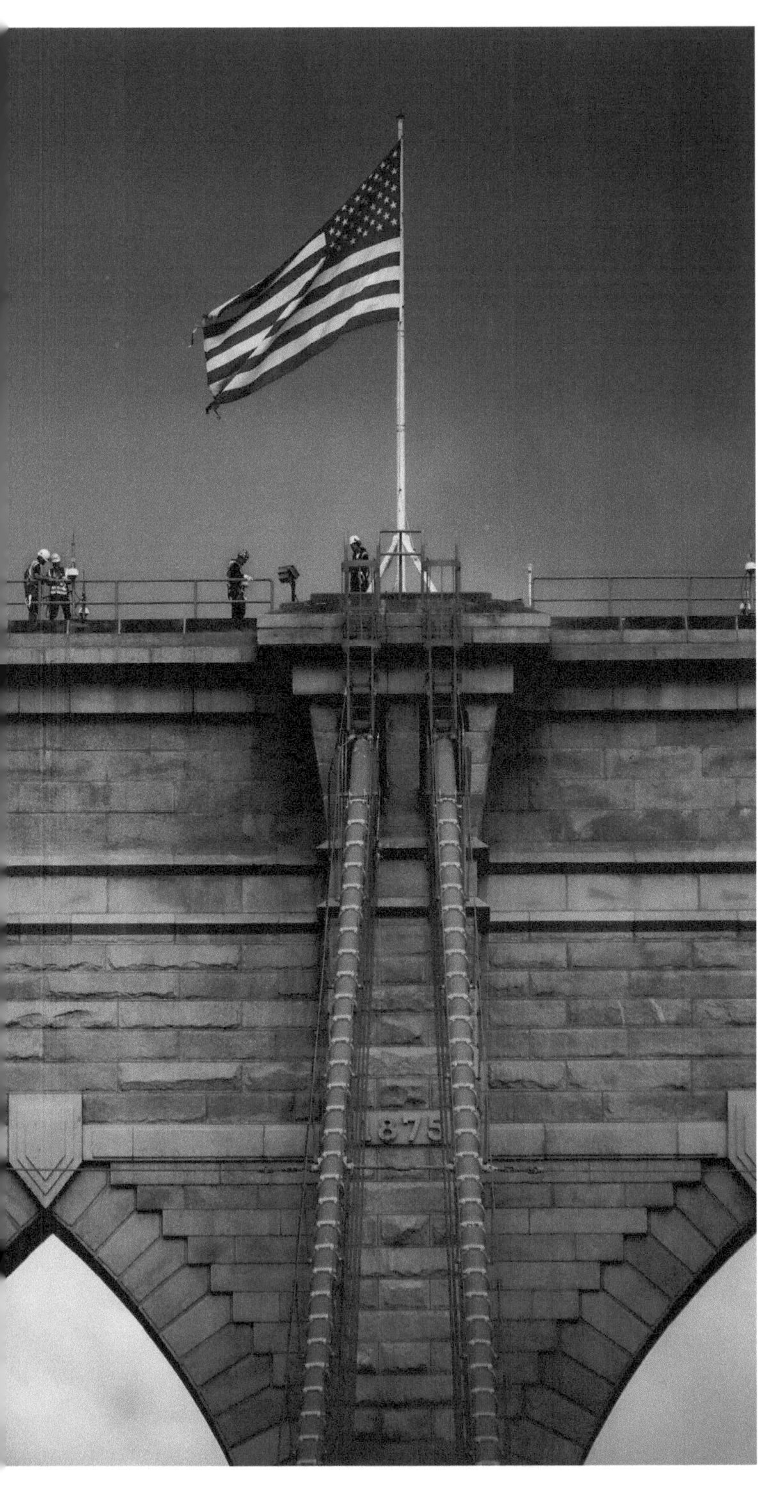

Hope rises where stone meets sky.

CH 2 . SOLITUDE IN MOTION

In New York, loneliness is rarely still.
It moves—across bridges, down stairwells,
through puddles reflecting the sky.

The city keeps its rhythm,
yet each person walks with a different weight:
some escaping, some approaching,
some simply searching for a breath that isn't chased by time.

To watch someone moving alone
is to recognize a version of ourselves—
quiet, unresolved, walking toward a direction
we have not yet named.

Every yellow streak is a note in New York's restless symphony.

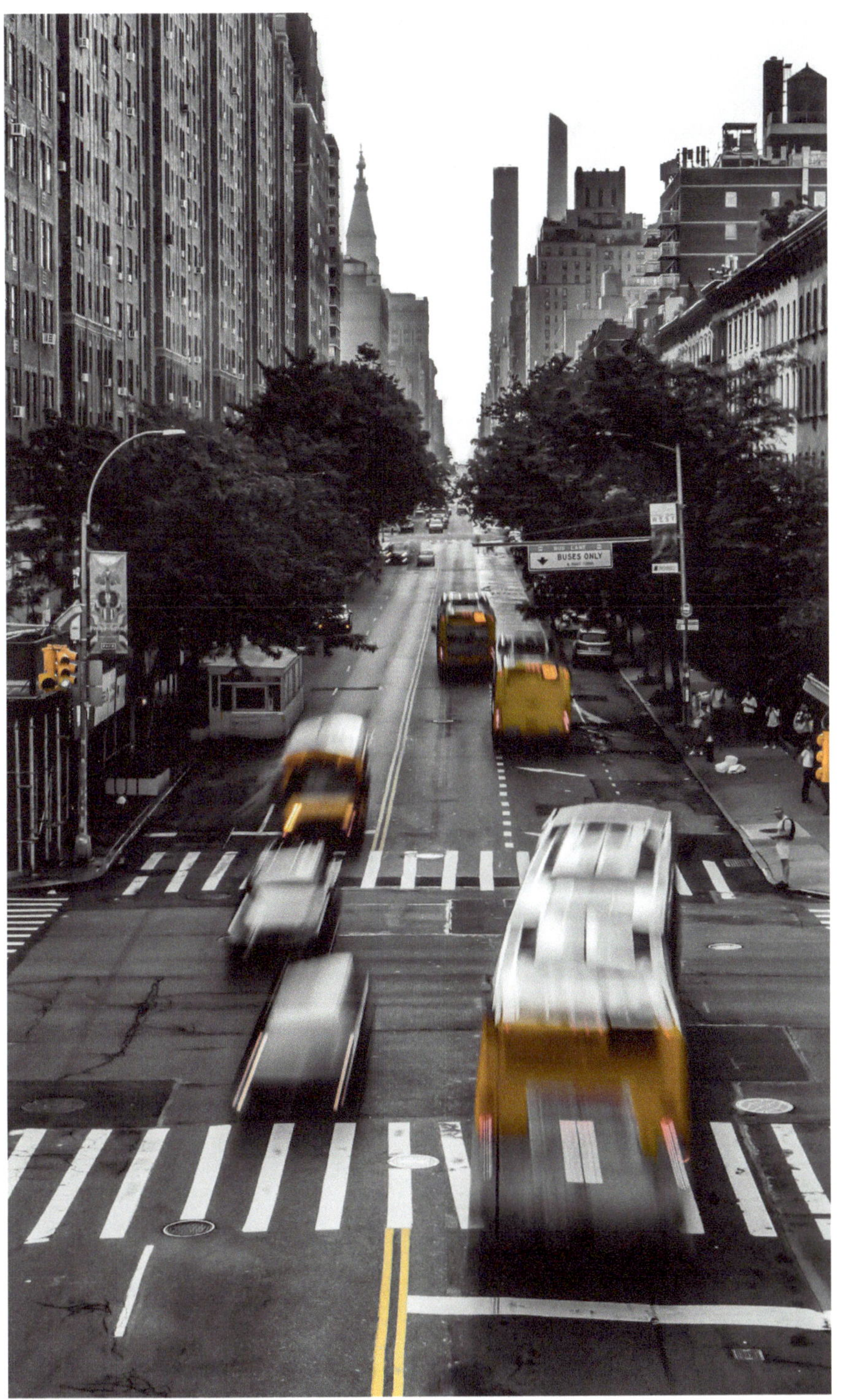

BUSES ONLY

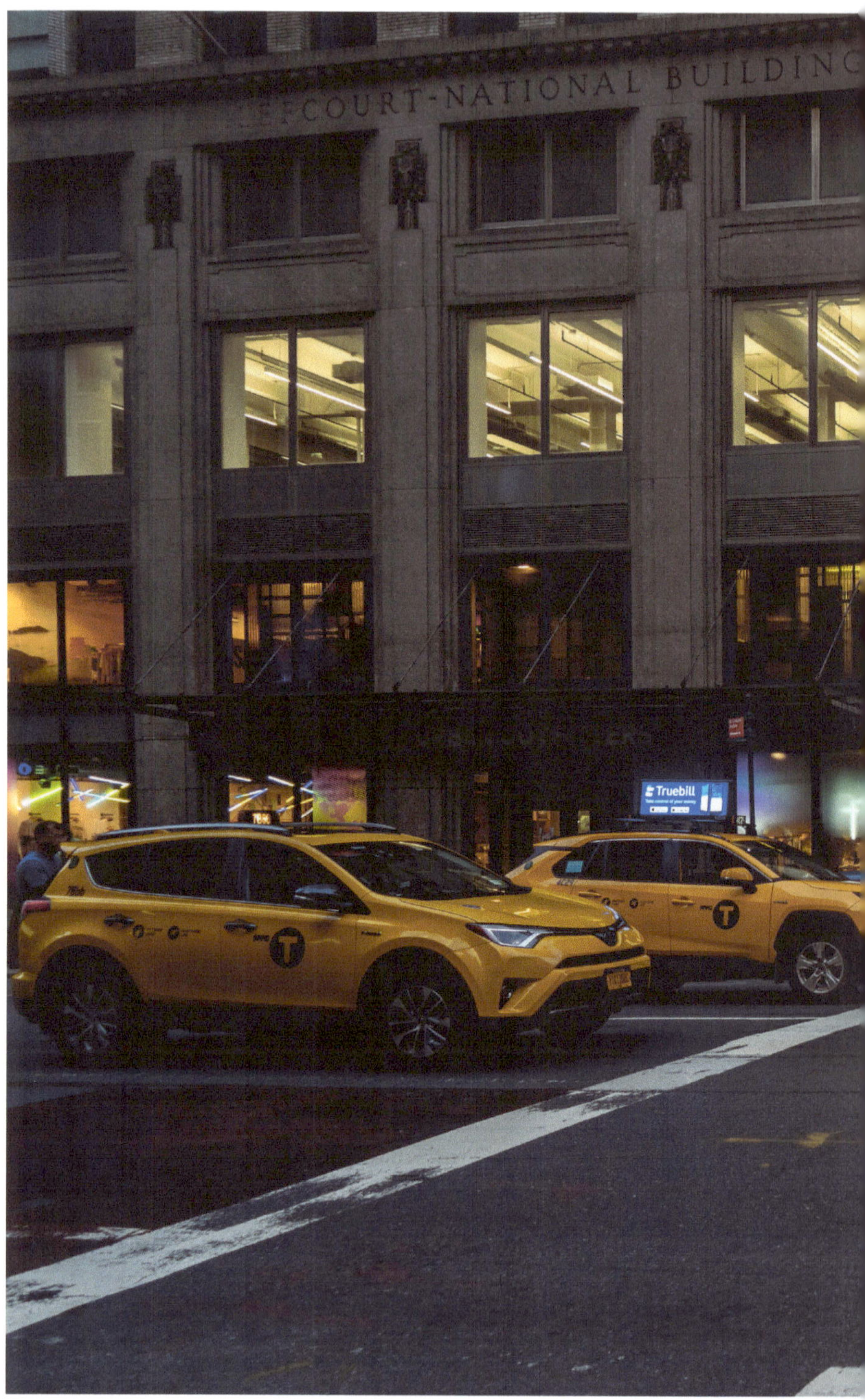

COURT-NATIONAL BUILDING
Truebill

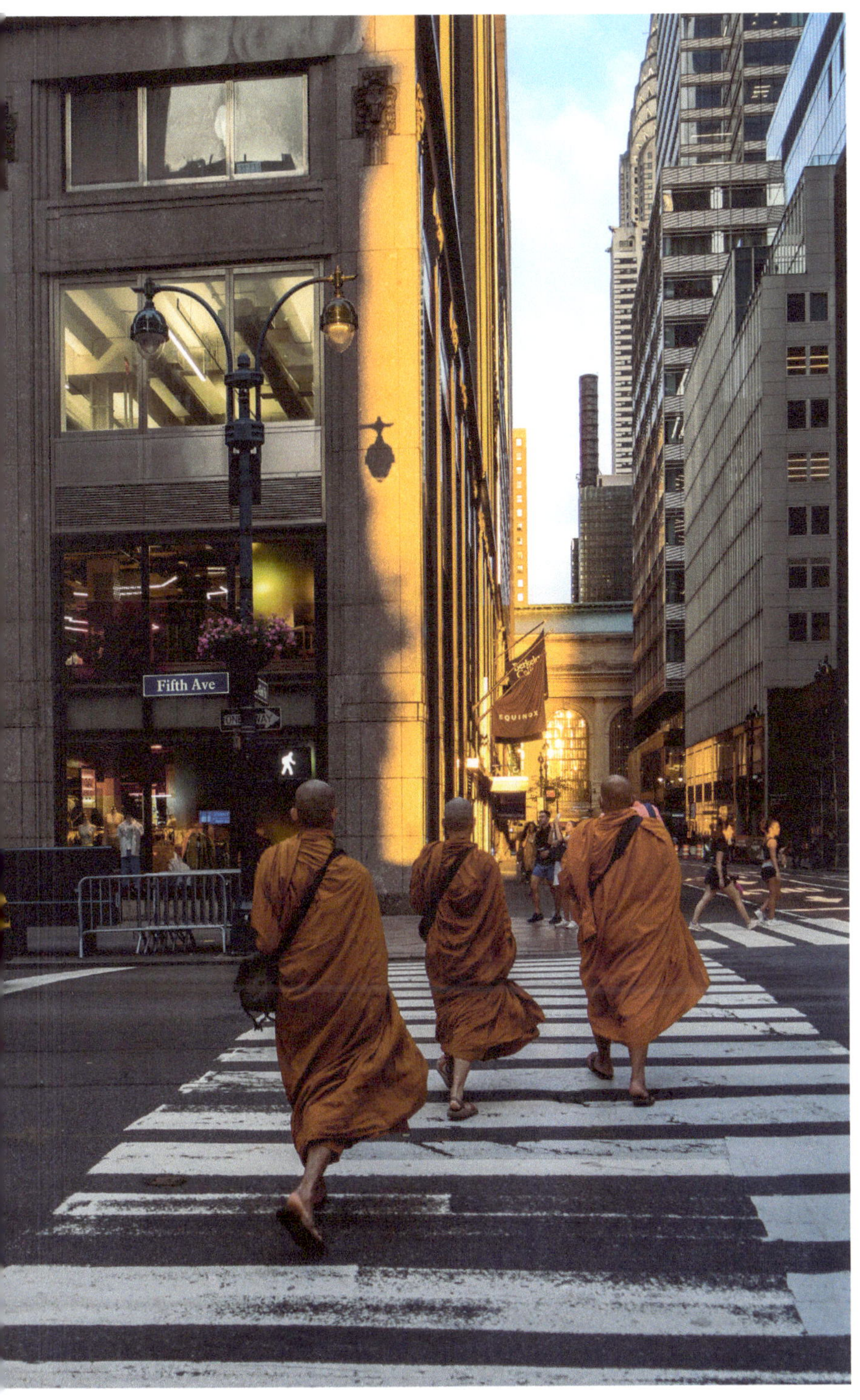

They move untouched by the city's weight and even the street holds its breath.

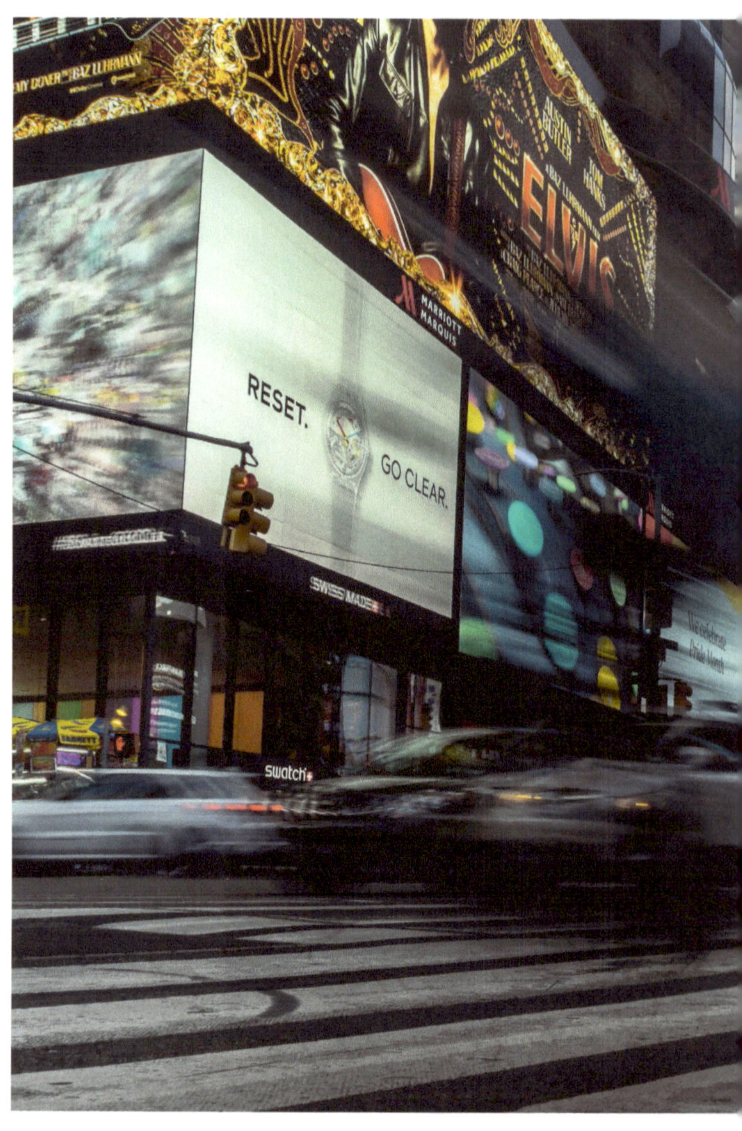

Where movement blurs, he remains.

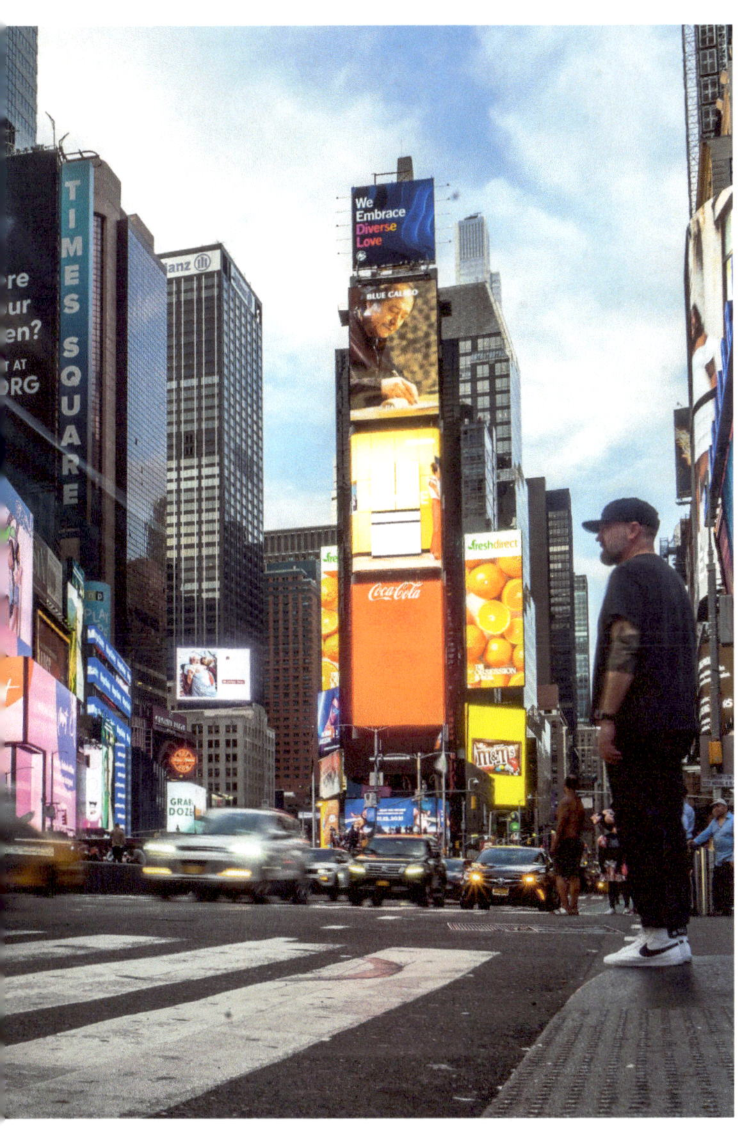
TIMES SQUARE
re
ur
en?
AT
ORG
Allianz
We
Embrace
Diverse
Love
BLUE CALIBO
freshdirect
Coca-Cola
m&m's
GRAB
DOZE

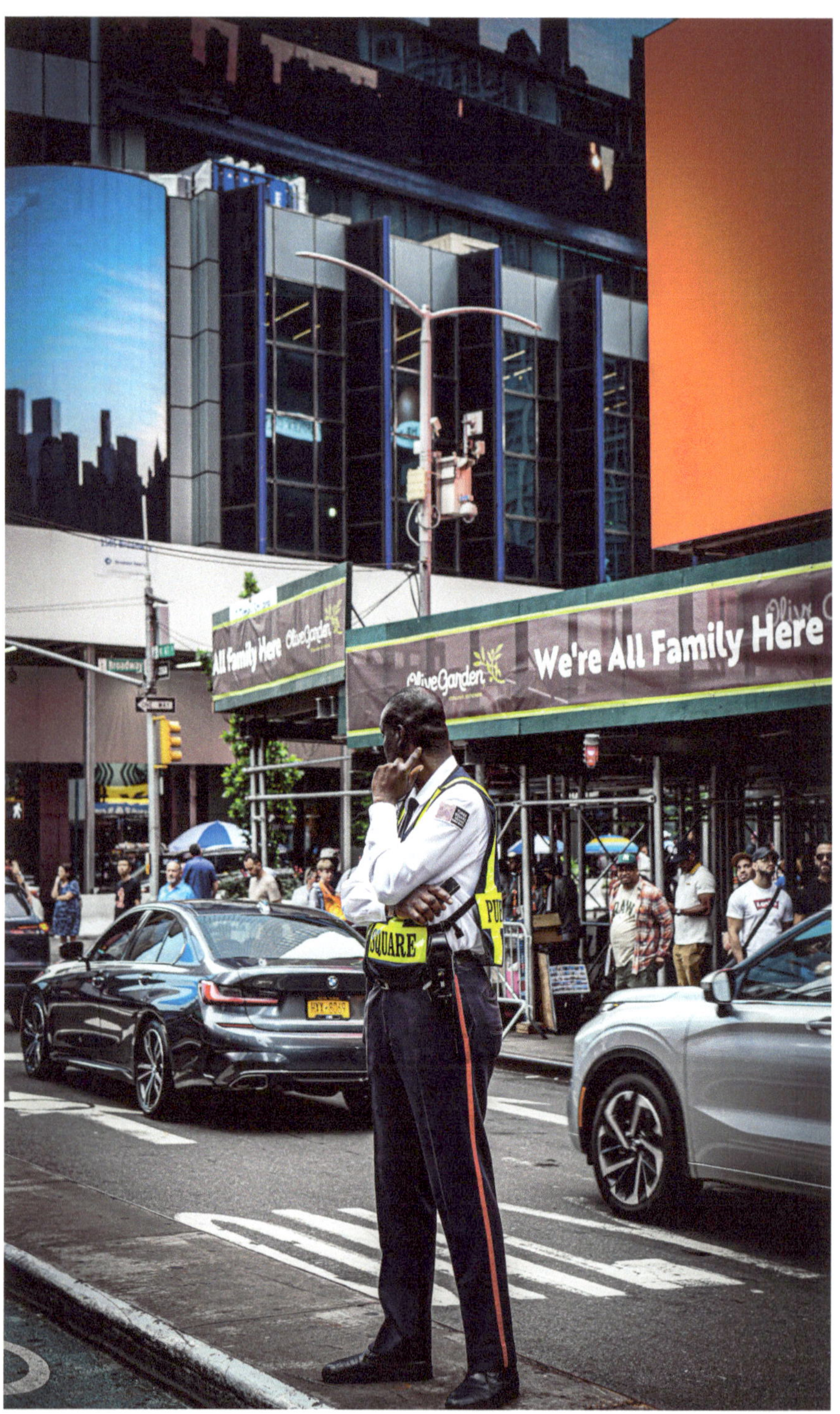
All Family Here
Olive Garden
We're All Family Here
Olive Garden
SQUARE
PUB

Order inside the chaos.

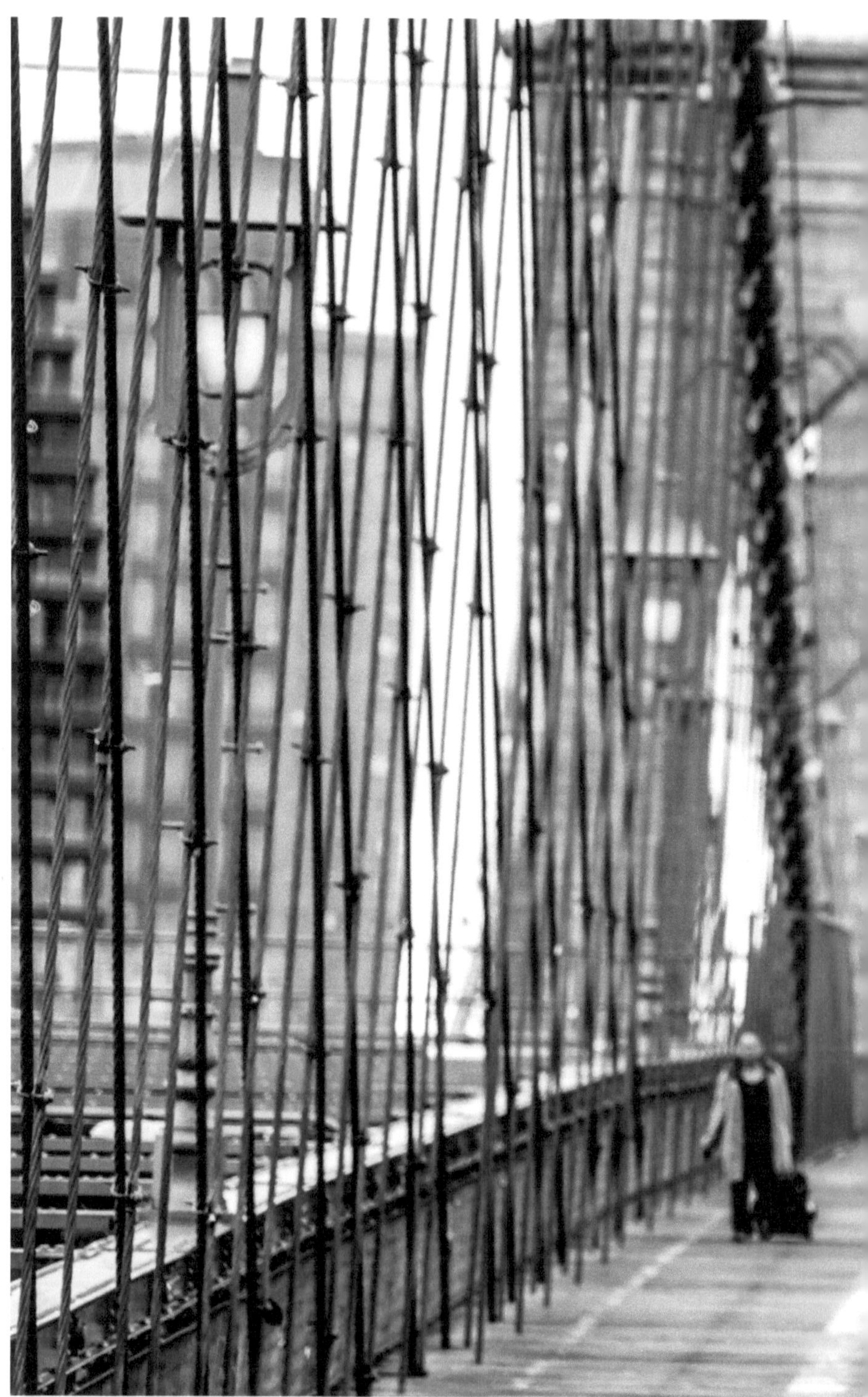

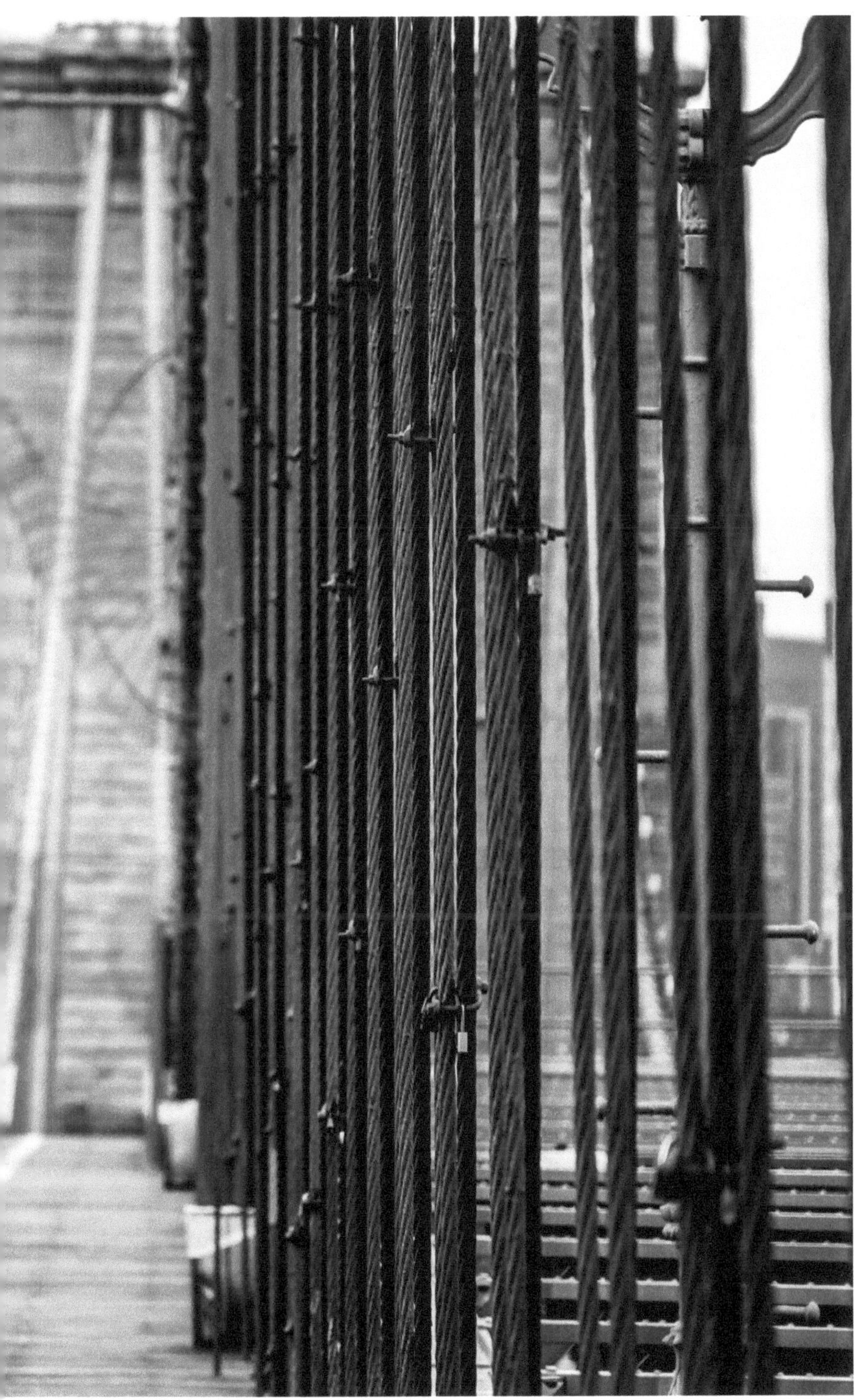

Wrapped in cables and silence, she keeps moving—because stopping was never an option.

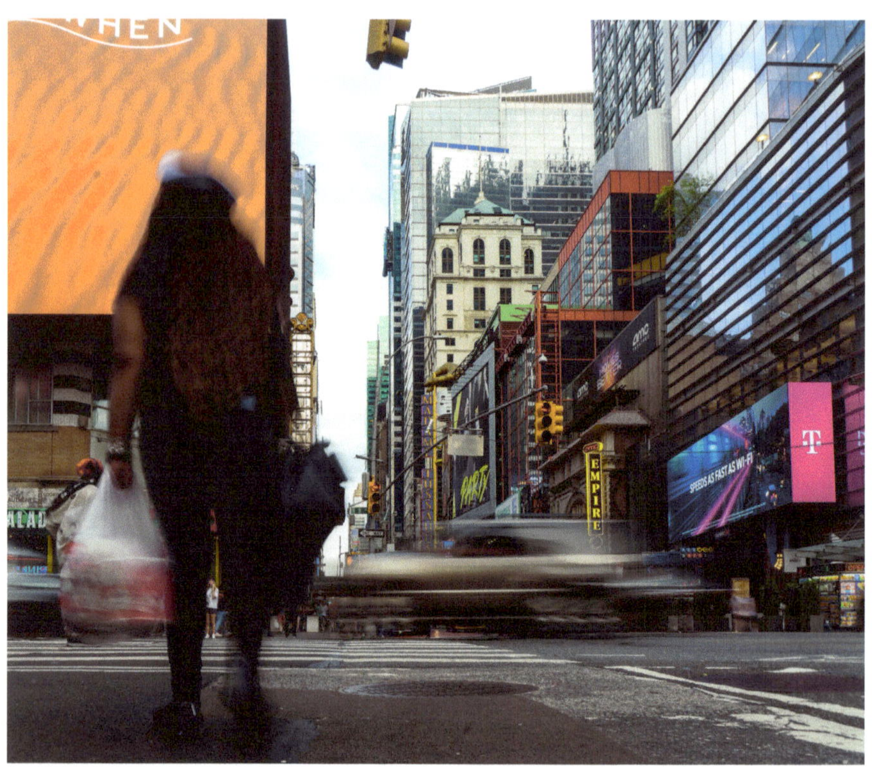

The real trial is the moment you must wait for your own heart to catch up.

Even the strongest steel beams can't hold the weight he carries today.

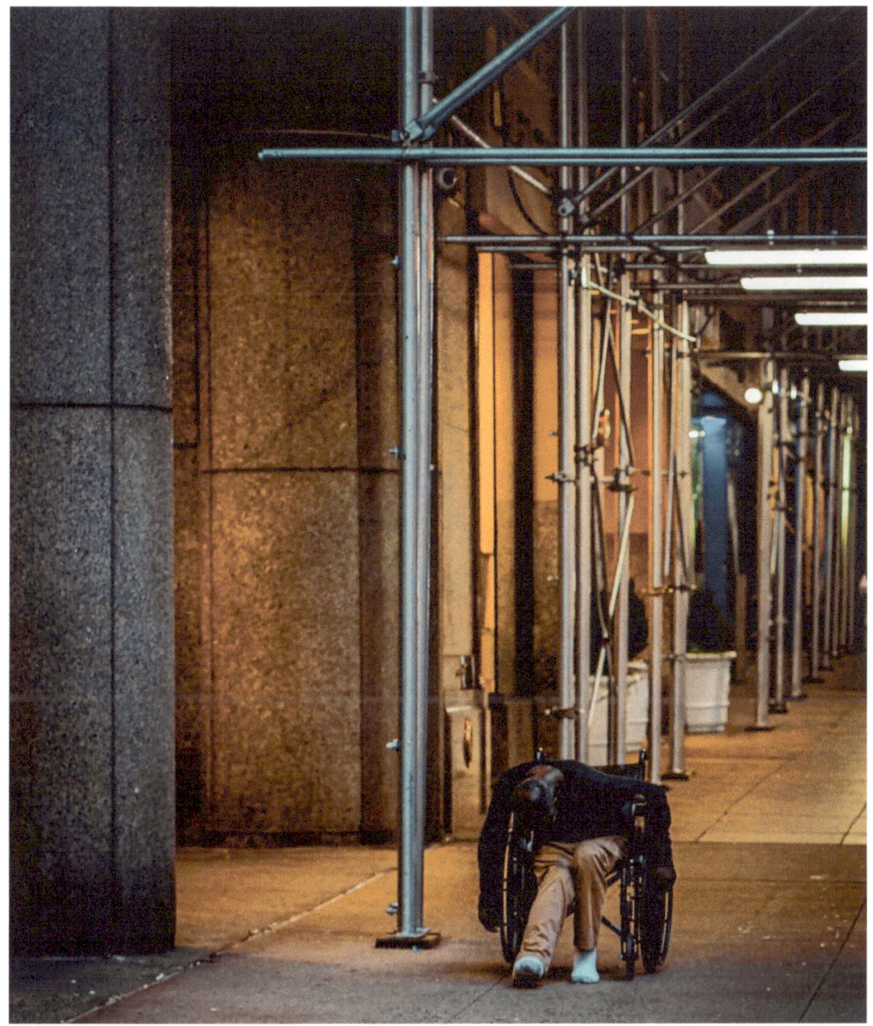

CH 3 . ECHOES OF THE CITY

In New York, buildings often speak before people do.
Stone, steel, and glass form a silent chronicle,
recording endless cycles of construction, collapse, and return.

Repetitive grids, cold reflections,
and uncompromising vertical lines
remind us that this city never slows for anyone's emotions.

Here, human presence is reduced to a footnote,
while the city moves like a tireless machine—
breathing, vibrating, echoing
through the narrow gaps between towers.

This chapter listens to New York at its quietest:
its order, its force, its distance.
Beneath those cold surfaces,
a pulse continues—unbroken.

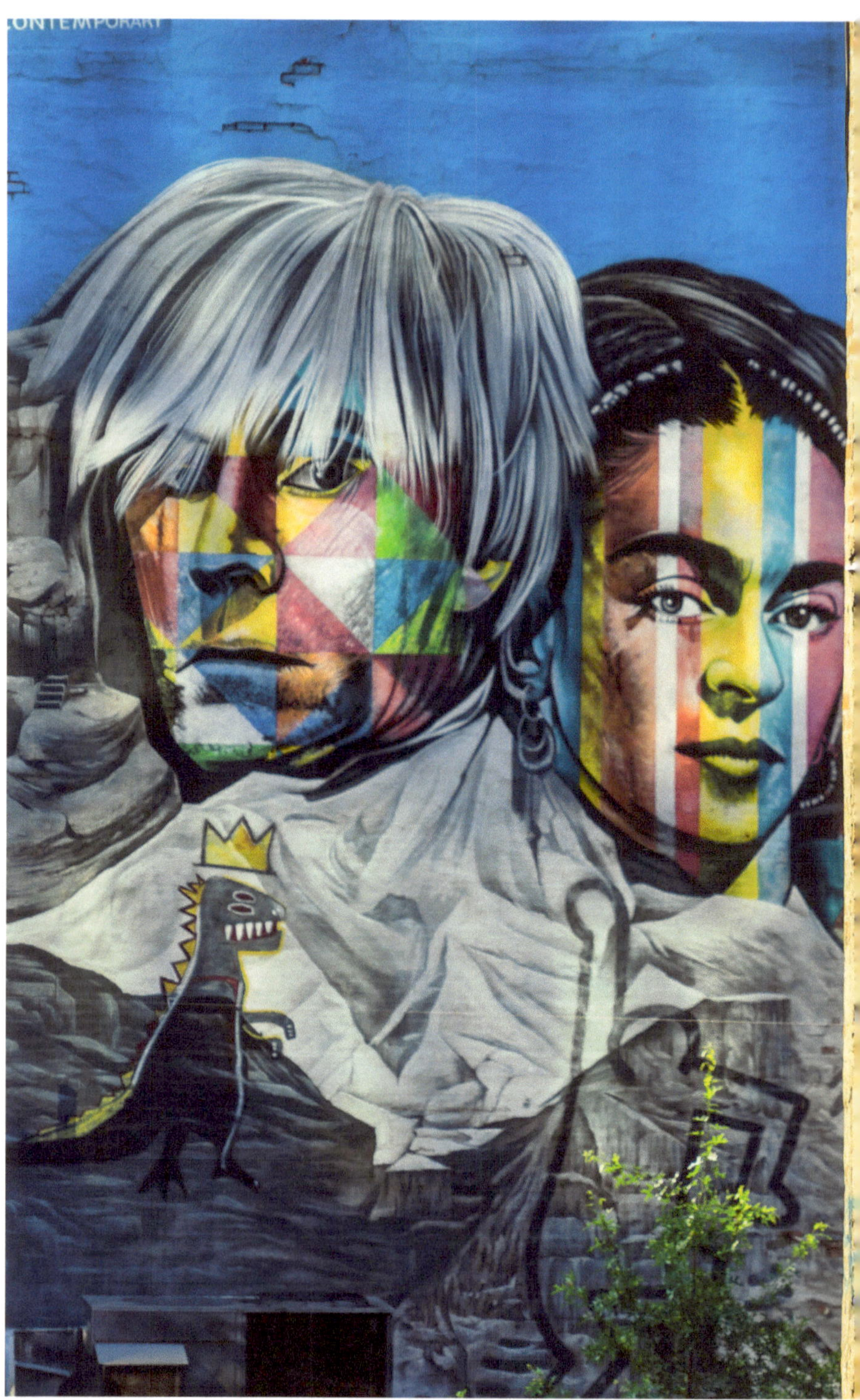

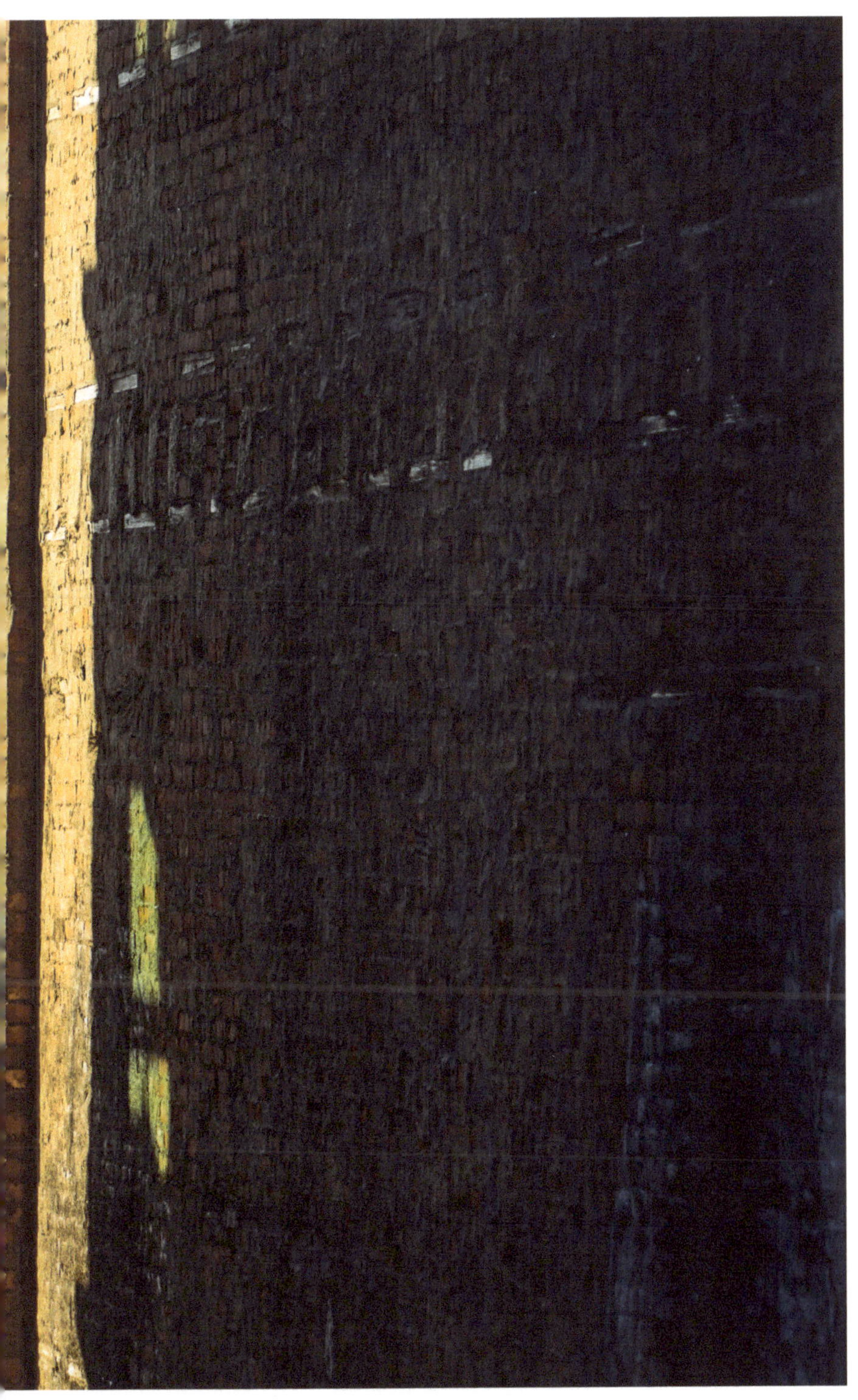

Faces on the wall speak truths we are too afraid to admit aloud.

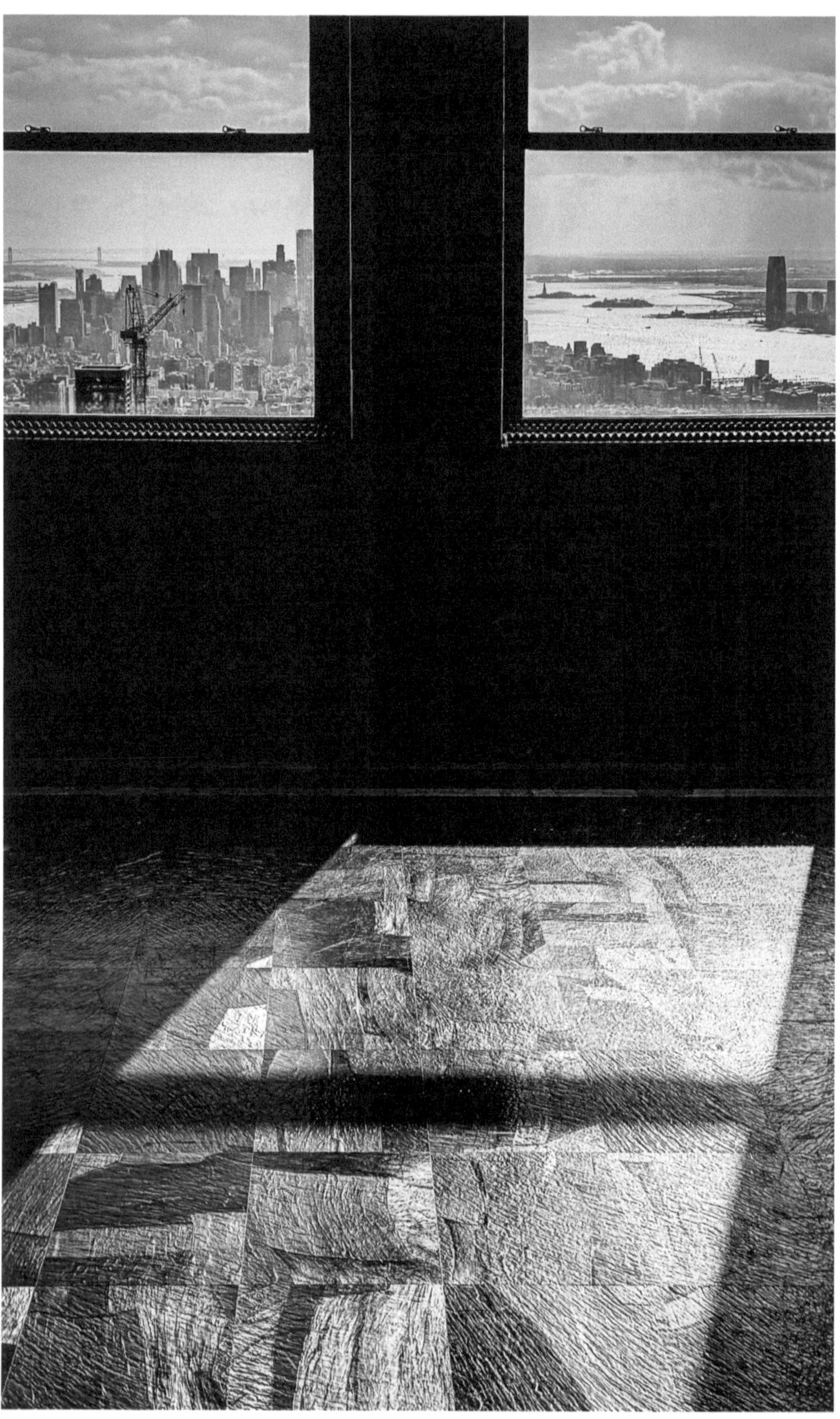

Between two windows, the city repeats itself—not louder, only deeper.

The city's colors shift like emotions we pretend not to feel.

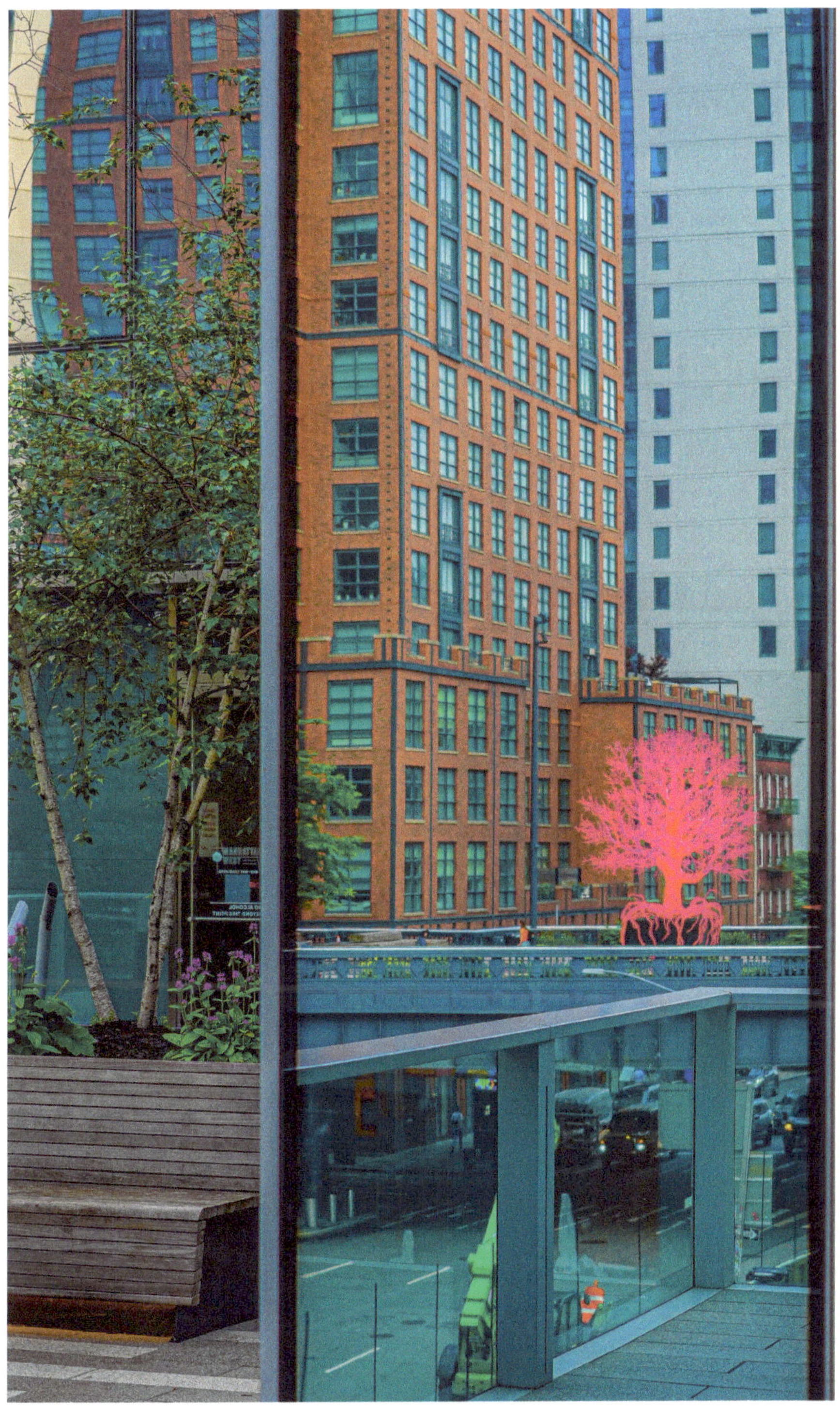

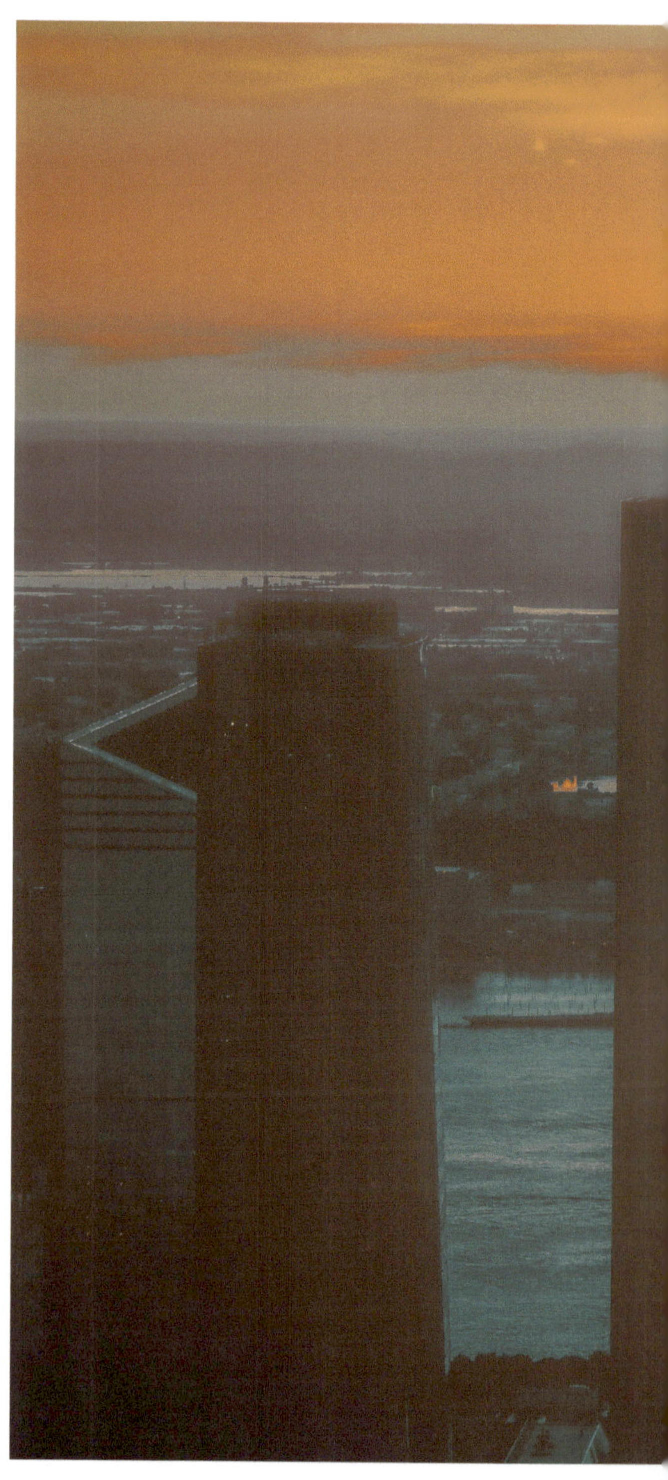

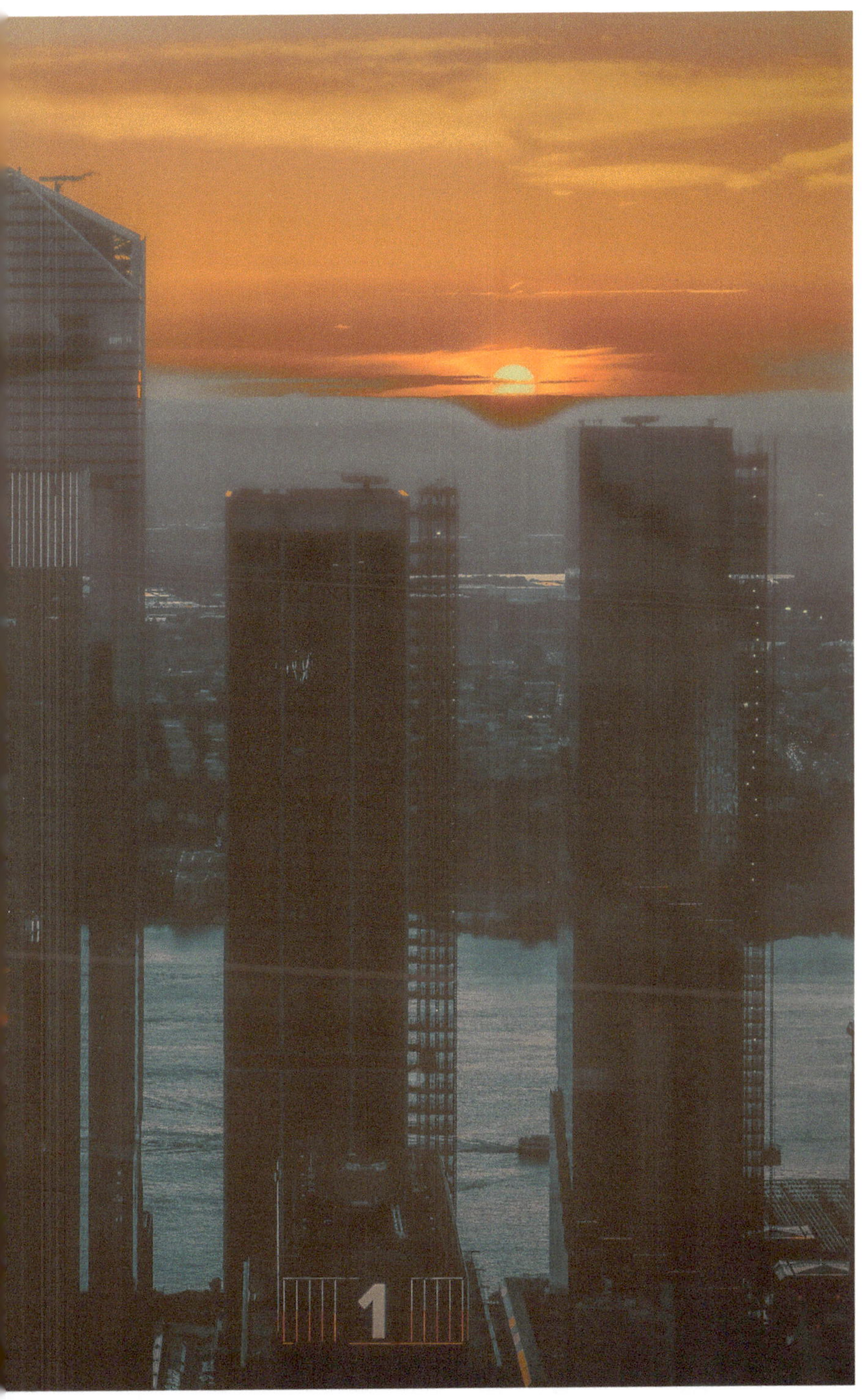
1

A silent witness watches the street, unmasked by the light.

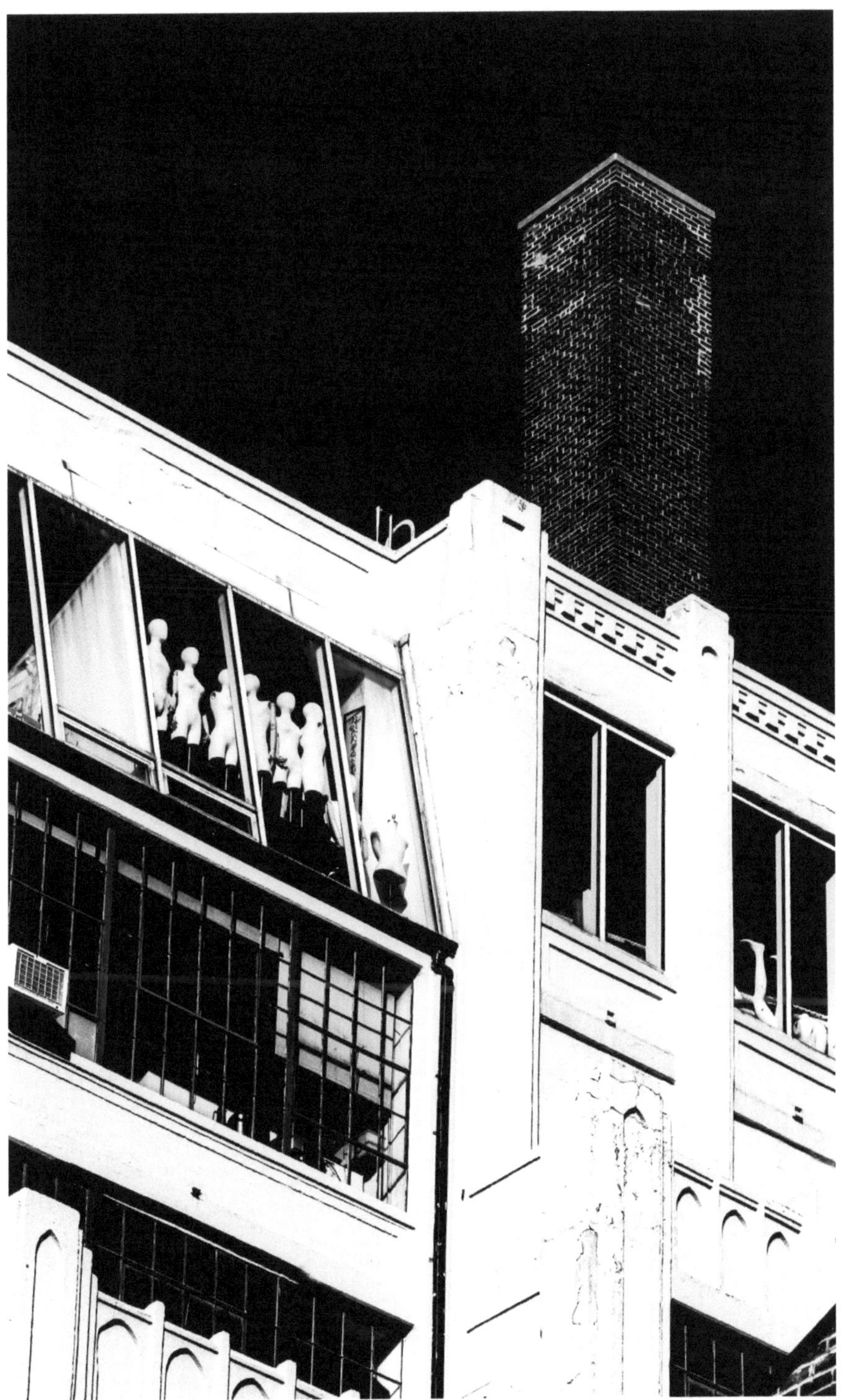

The city crowns its quiet monarch, framed by steel and sky.

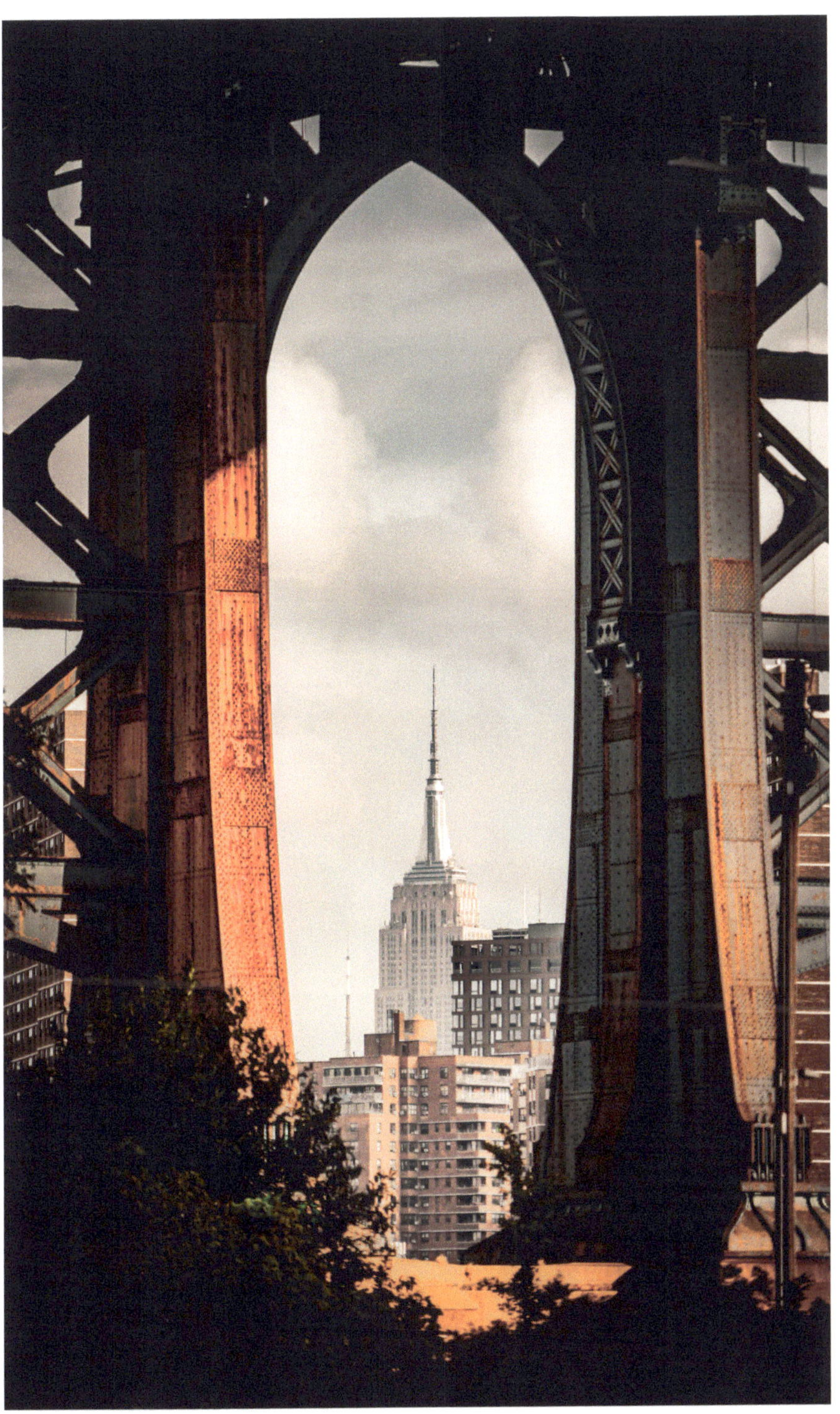

CH 4 . HUMAN TRACES

In New York, distance is measured not in meters
but in glances, footsteps, and silences.

This chapter searches for the gestures the city nearly forgets:
a pause by a wall,
a hesitant shadow under a subway beam,
a small wave toward a shore that may never answer back.

These traces remind us that every pause
is a secret pact with the city —
a moment of being seen,
even when no one is watching.

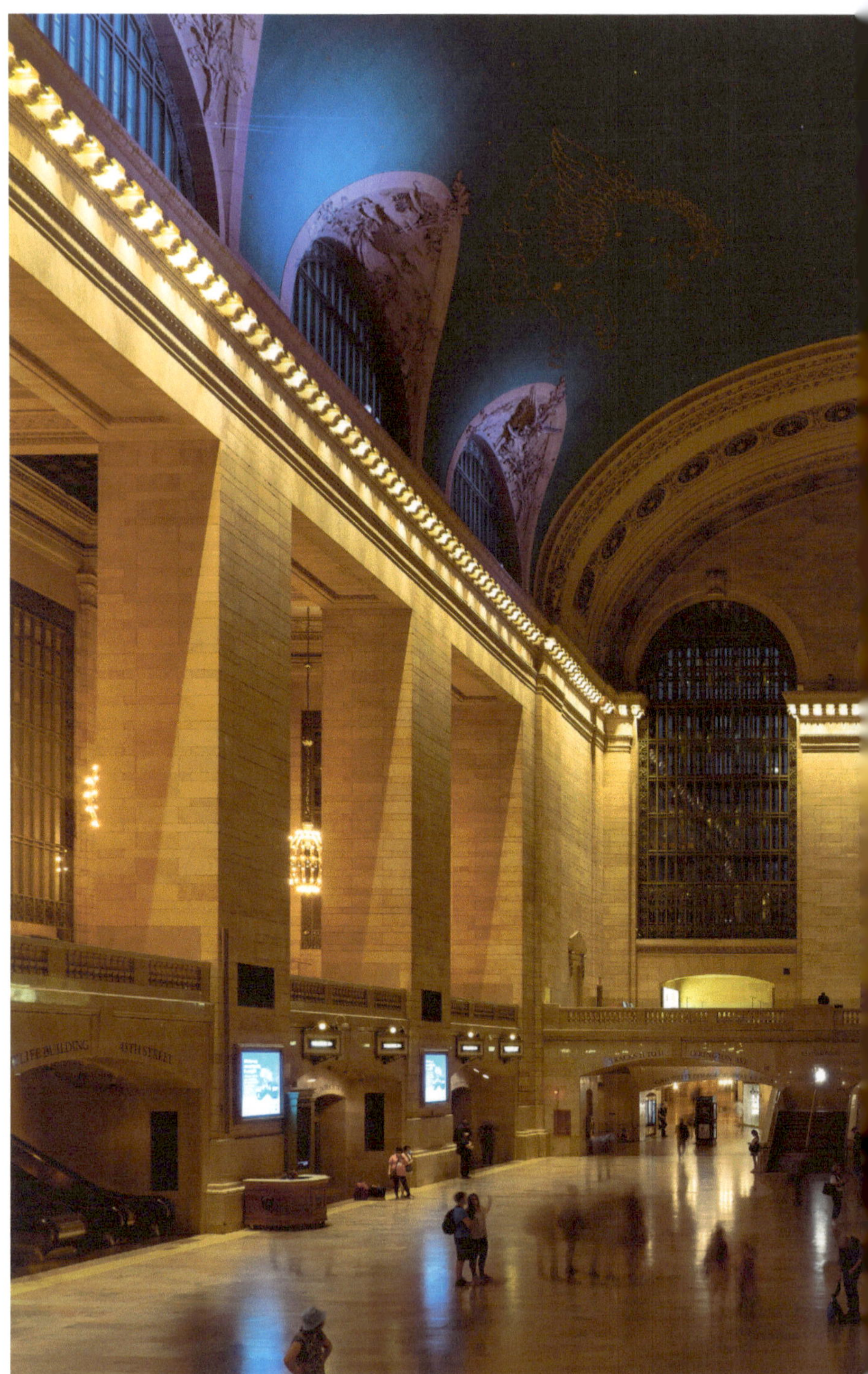

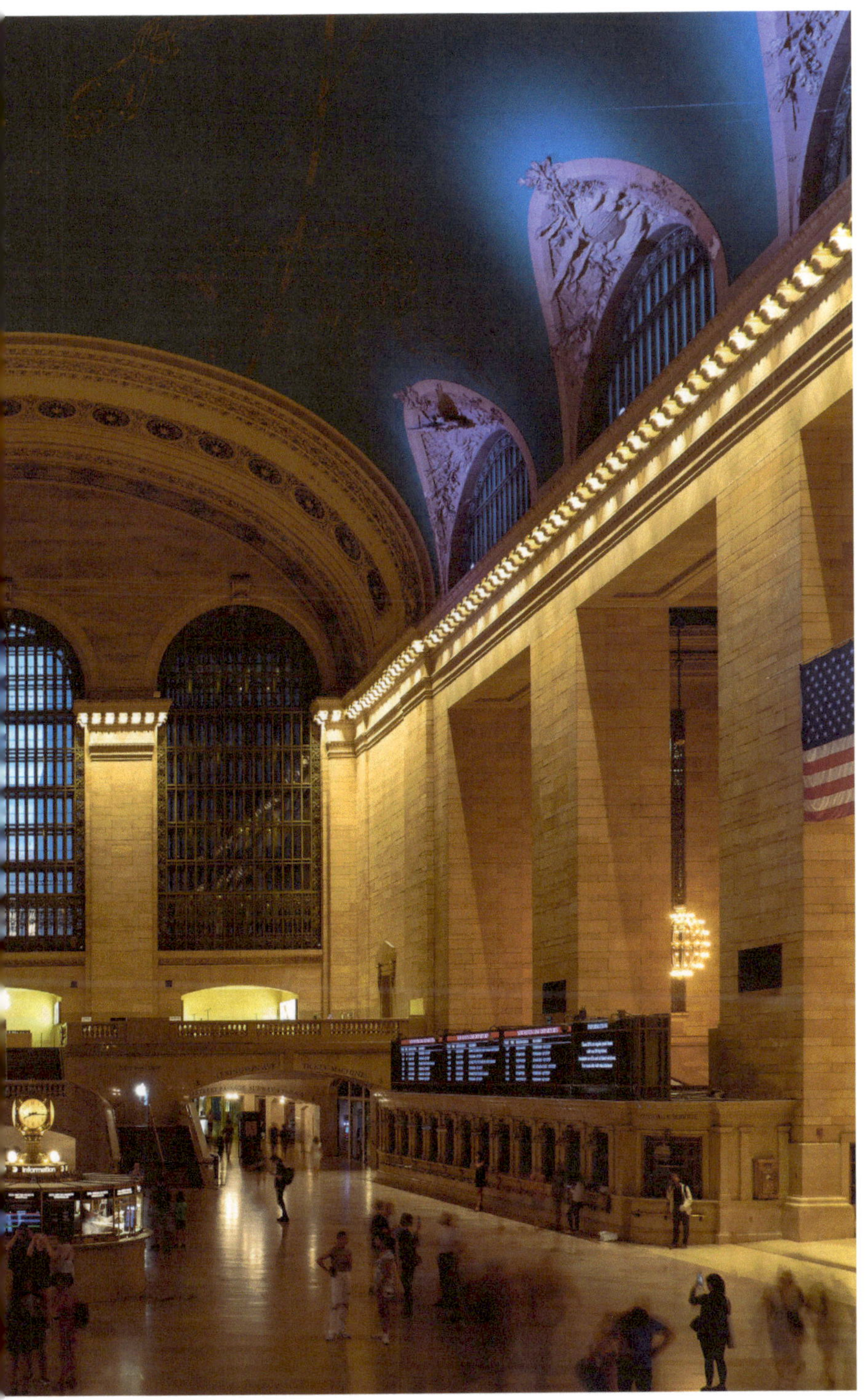

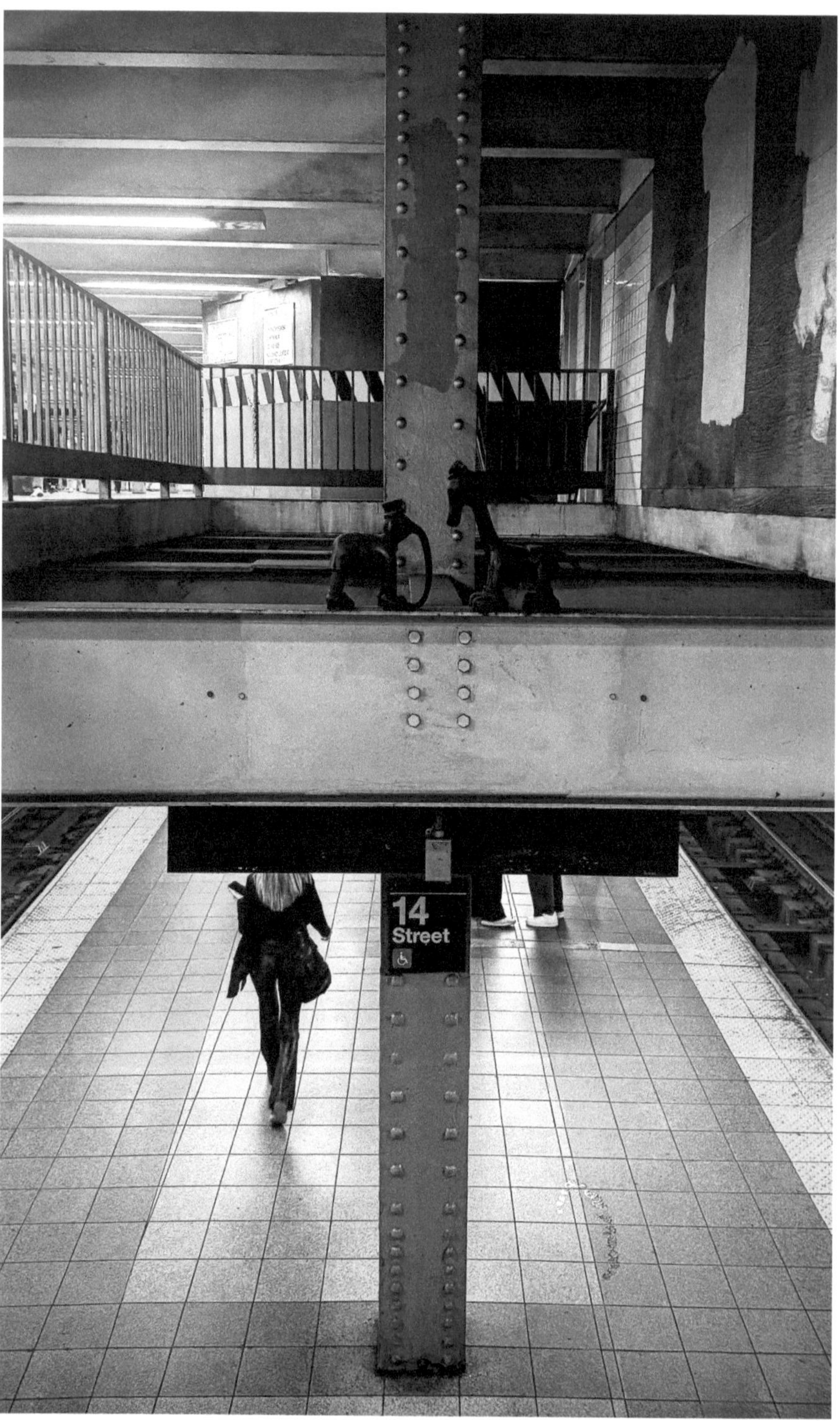
14
Street

Beneath the tracks, every step sounds like a decision made twice.

A cathedral of motion where every stranger becomes part of the same quiet choreography.

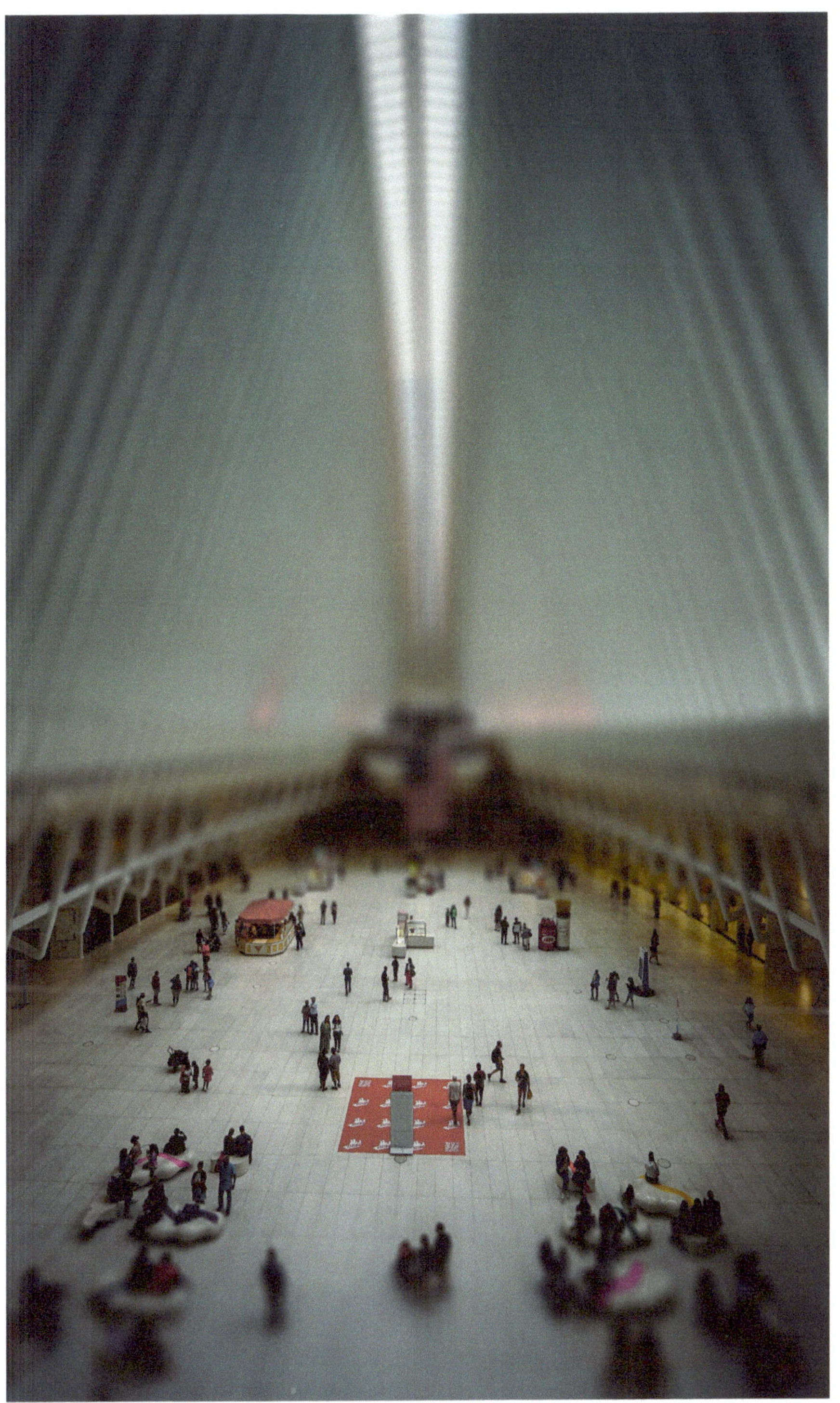

At the city's loudest crossroads, loneliness still finds a place to rest.

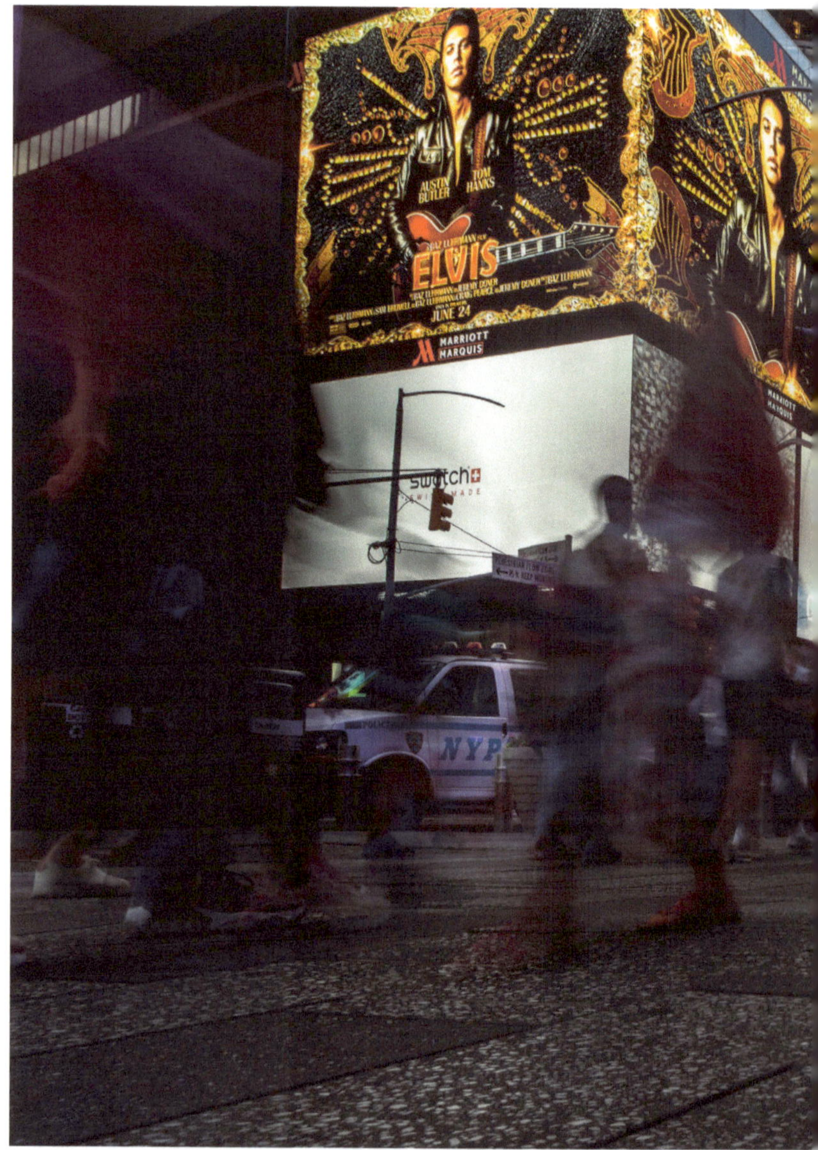

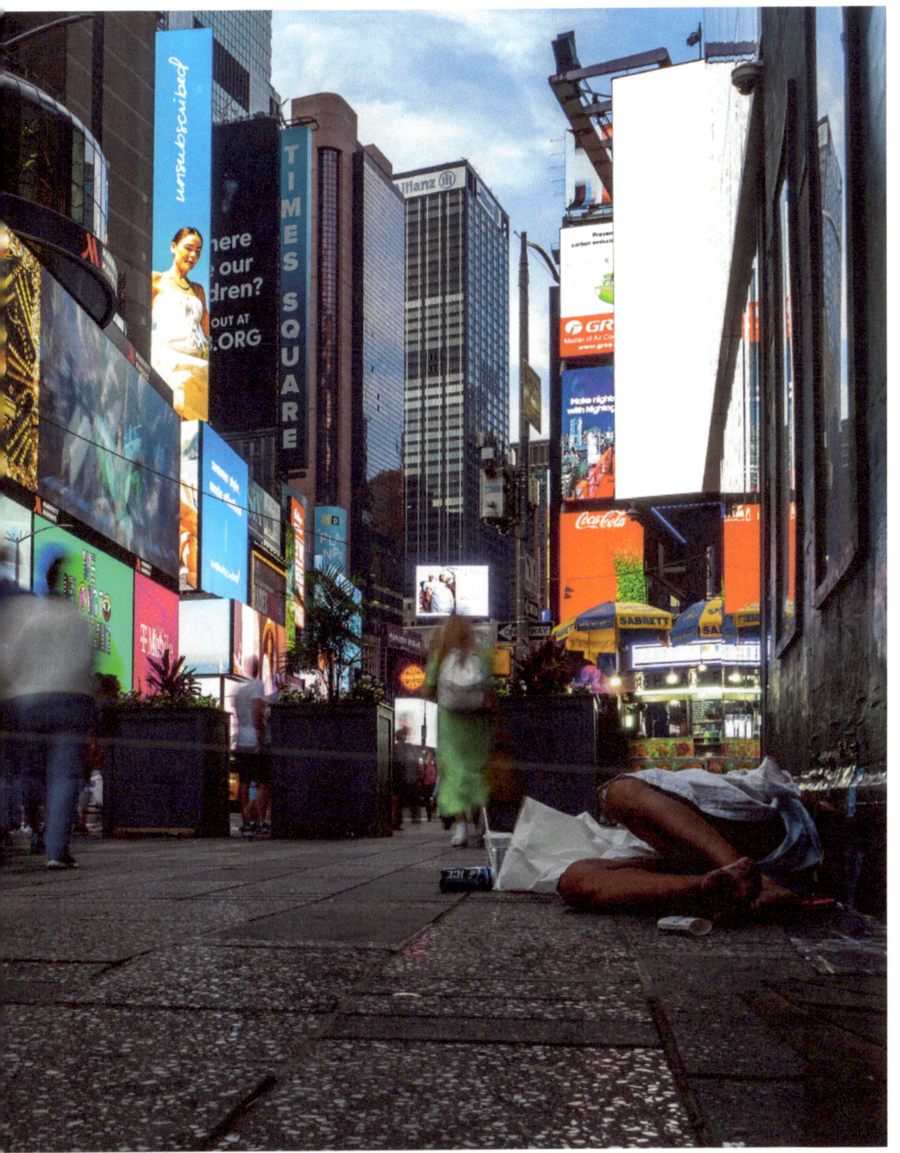

unsubscribed
here
e our
dren?
OUT AT
.ORG
TIMES SQUARE
Allianz
Coca-Cola
SABRETT
ICE

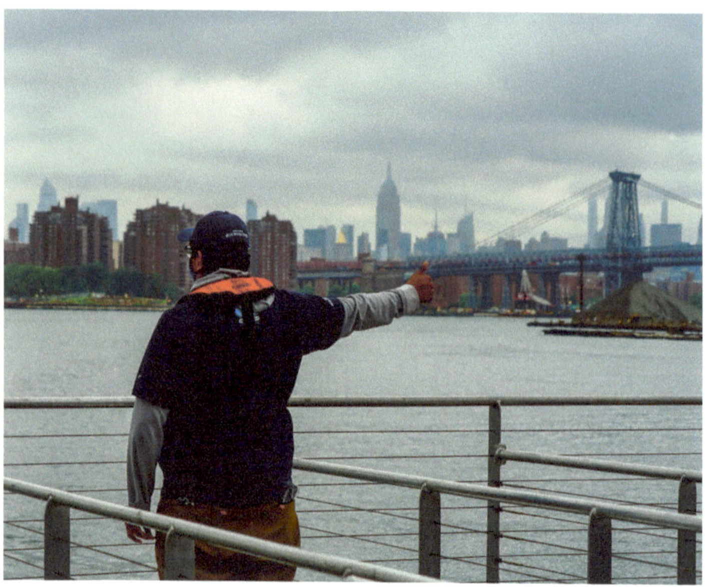

He signals to the city, not for someone—just because duty never waits.

Before the bell rings, two worlds share a moment no one else will ever see.

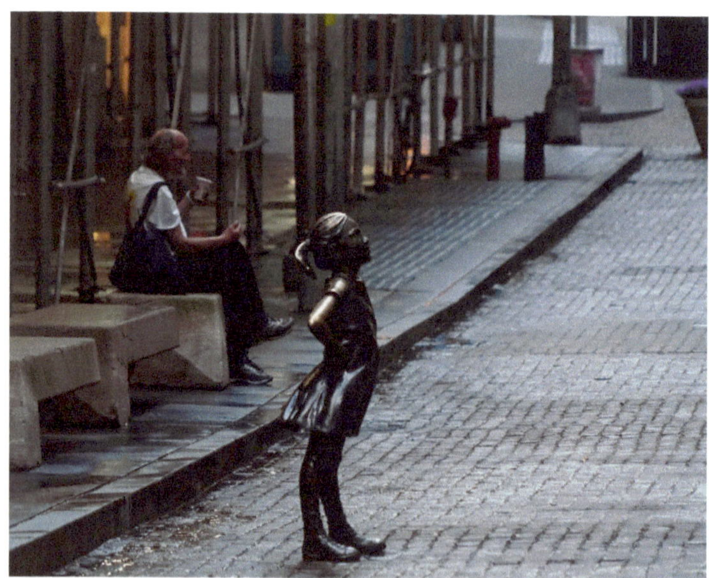

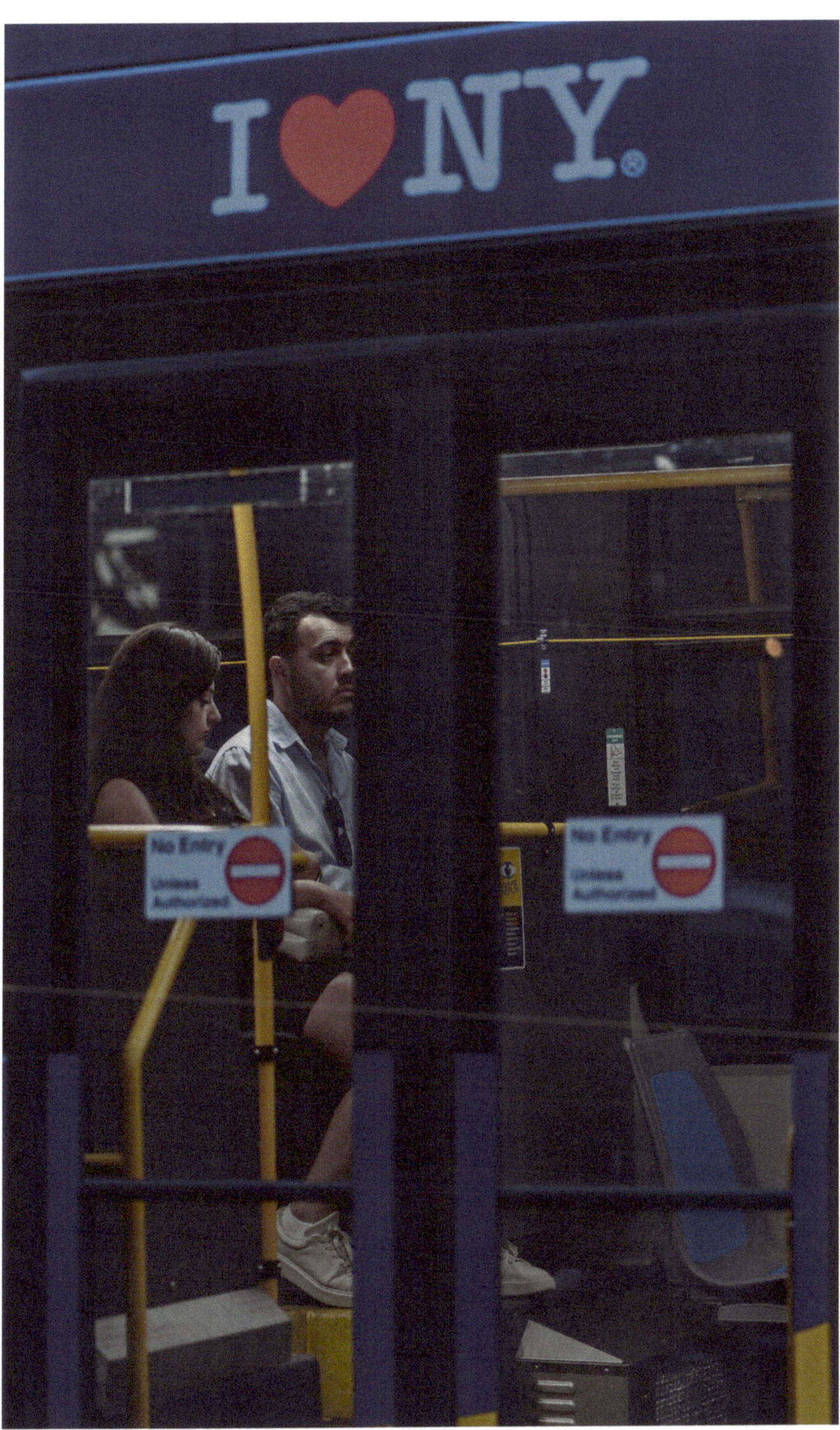

Lovers or Strangers? But the city has already placed a heart between them.

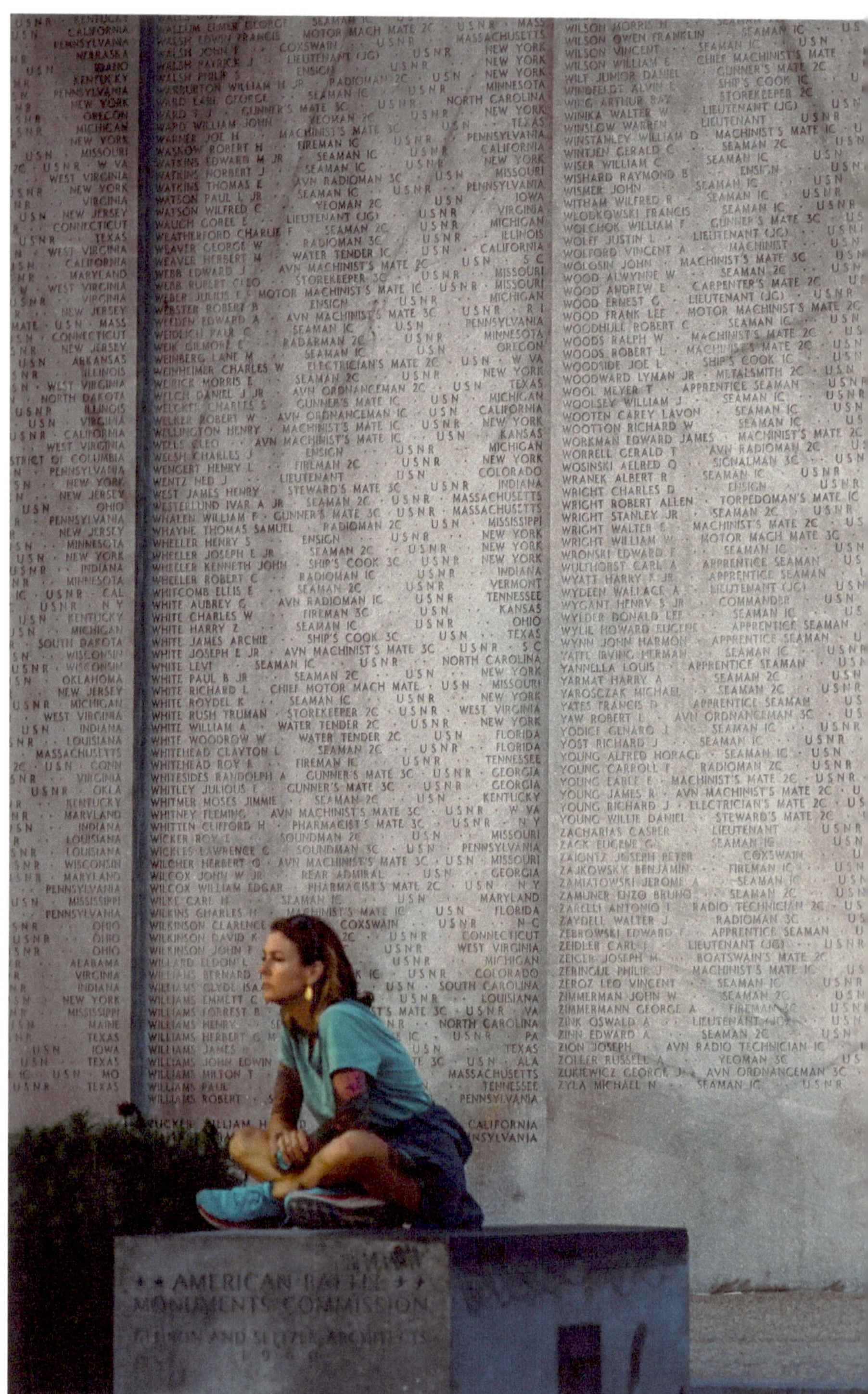

BALLUM ELMER GEORGE · SEAMAN 1C · USNR · MASS
WALSH EDWIN FRANCIS · MOTOR MACH MATE 2C · USNR · MASSACHUSETTS
WALSH JOHN J · COXSWAIN · USNR · NEW YORK
WALSH PATRICK J · LIEUTENANT (JG) · USNR · NEW YORK
WALSH PHILIP S · ENSIGN · USNR · NEW YORK
WARBURTON WILLIAM H JR · RADIOMAN 2C · USN · MINNESOTA
WARD CARL GEORGE · SEAMAN 1C · USNR · NORTH CAROLINA
WARD S J · GUNNER'S MATE 3C · USNR · NEW YORK
WARD WILLIAM JOHN · YEOMAN 2C · USN · NEW YORK
WARNER JOE H · MACHINIST'S MATE 3C · USNR · PENNSYLVANIA
WASNOW ROBERT H · FIREMAN 1C · USNR · CALIFORNIA
WATKINS EDWARD M JR · SEAMAN 1C · USNR · NEW YORK
WATKINS NORBERT J · SEAMAN 1C · USNR · MISSOURI
WATKINS THOMAS E · AVN RADIOMAN 3C · USNR · PENNSYLVANIA
WATSON PAUL L JR · SEAMAN 1C · USNR · IOWA
WATSON WILFRED C · YEOMAN 2C · USN · VIRGINIA
WAUGH GOREE E · LIEUTENANT (JG) · USNR · MICHIGAN
WEATHERFORD CHARLIE F · SEAMAN 2C · USNR · ILLINOIS
WEAVER GEORGE W · RADIOMAN 3C · USN · CALIFORNIA
WEAVER HERBERT M · WATER TENDER 1C · USN · S C
WEBB EDWARD J · AVN MACHINIST'S MATE 2C · USNR · MISSOURI
WEBB RUPERT CLEO · STOREKEEPER 3C · USNR · MISSOURI
WEBER JULIUS E · MOTOR MACHINIST'S MATE 1C · USNR · MICHIGAN
WEBSTER ROBERT B · ENSIGN · USNR · R I
WEEDEN EDWARD A · AVN MACHINIST'S MATE 3C · USN · PENNSYLVANIA
WEIDLICH PAUL G · RADARMAN 2C · USNR · MINNESOTA
WEIR GILMORE C · SEAMAN 1C · USN · OREGON
WEINBERG LANE M · ELECTRICIAN'S MATE 2C · USN · W VA
WEINHEIMER CHARLES W · SEAMAN 2C · USNR · NEW YORK
WEIRICK MORRIS E · AVN ORDNANCEMAN 2C · USN · TEXAS
WELCH DANIEL J JR · GUNNER'S MATE 1C · USN · MICHIGAN
WELCKER CHARLES S · AVN ORDNANCEMAN 1C · USN · CALIFORNIA
WELKER ROBERT W · MACHINIST'S MATE 1C · USN · NEW YORK
WELLINGTON HENRY · AVN MACHINIST'S MATE 1C · USN · KANSAS
WELLS CLEO · ENSIGN · USNR · MICHIGAN
WELSH CHARLES J · FIREMAN 2C · USNR · NEW YORK
WENGERT HENRY L · LIEUTENANT · USN · COLORADO
WENTZ NED J · STEWARD'S MATE 3C · USNR · INDIANA
WEST JAMES HENRY · SEAMAN 2C · USNR · MASSACHUSETTS
WESTERLUND IVAR A JR · GUNNER'S MATE 3C · USNR · MASSACHUSETTS
WHALEN WILLIAM F · RADIOMAN 2C · USN · MISSISSIPPI
WHAYNE THOMAS SAMUEL · ENSIGN · USNR · NEW YORK
WHEELER HENRY S · SEAMAN 2C · USNR · NEW YORK
WHEELER JOSEPH E JR · SHIP'S COOK 3C · USNR · NEW YORK
WHEELER KENNETH JOHN · RADIOMAN 1C · USNR · INDIANA
WHEELER ROBERT C · SEAMAN 2C · USNR · VERMONT
WHITCOMB ELLIS E · AVN RADIOMAN 1C · USNR · TENNESSEE
WHITE AUBREY G · FIREMAN 3C · USN · KANSAS
WHITE CHARLES W · SEAMAN 1C · USNR · OHIO
WHITE HARRY Z · SHIP'S COOK 3C · USN · TEXAS
WHITE JAMES ARCHIE · AVN MACHINIST'S MATE 3C · USNR · S C
WHITE JOSEPH E JR · SEAMAN 1C · USNR · NORTH CAROLINA
WHITE LEVI · SEAMAN 2C · USN · NEW YORK
WHITE PAUL B JR · CHIEF MOTOR MACH MATE · USN · MISSOURI
WHITE RICHARD L · SEAMAN 1C · USNR · NEW YORK
WHITE ROYDEL K · STOREKEEPER 2C · USNR · WEST VIRGINIA
WHITE RUSH TRUMAN · WATER TENDER 2C · USNR · NEW YORK
WHITE WILLIAM A · WATER TENDER 2C · USN · FLORIDA
WHITE WOODROW W · SEAMAN 2C · USNR · FLORIDA
WHITEHEAD CLAYTON L · FIREMAN 1C · USNR · TENNESSEE
WHITEHEAD ROY E · GUNNER'S MATE 3C · USNR · GEORGIA
WHITESIDES RANDOLPH A · GUNNER'S MATE 3C · USNR · GEORGIA
WHITLEY JULIOUS E · SEAMAN 2C · USN · KENTUCKY
WHITMER MOSES JIMMIE · AVN MACHINIST'S MATE 3C · USNR · W VA
WHITNEY FLEMING · PHARMACIST'S MATE 3C · USNR · N Y
WHITTEN CLIFFORD H · SOUNDMAN 2C · USN · MISSOURI
WICKER ROY E · SOUNDMAN 3C · USN · PENNSYLVANIA
WICKLES LAWRENCE G · AVN MACHINIST'S MATE 3C · USN · MISSOURI
WILCHER HERBERT O · REAR ADMIRAL · USN · GEORGIA
WILCOX JOHN W JR · PHARMACIST'S MATE 2C · USN · N Y
WILCOX WILLIAM EDGAR · SEAMAN 1C · USN · MARYLAND
WILKE CARL H · MACHINIST'S MATE 1C · USN · FLORIDA
WILKINS CHARLES H · COXSWAIN · USNR · N C
WILKINSON CLARENCE · SEAMAN 1C · USNR · CONNECTICUT
WILKINSON DAVID K · SEAMAN 1C · USNR · WEST VIRGINIA
WILKINSON JOHN F · SEAMAN 1C · USN · MICHIGAN
WILLARD ELDON L · SEAMAN 1C · USNR · COLORADO
WILLIAMS BERNARD · SEAMAN 1C · USN · SOUTH CAROLINA
WILLIAMS CLYDE ISAAC · SEAMAN 1C · USNR · LOUISIANA
WILLIAMS EMMETT C · MACHINIST'S MATE 3C · USNR · VA
WILLIAMS FORREST · SEAMAN 1C · USNR · NORTH CAROLINA
WILLIAMS HENRY · SEAMAN 1C · USN · TEXAS
WILLIAMS HERBERT G M · SEAMAN 1C · USNR · PA
WILLIAMS JAMES · SEAMAN 1C · USN · TEXAS
WILLIAMS JOHN EDWIN · SEAMAN 3C · USN · ALA
WILLIAMS MILTON T · SEAMAN 1C · USN · MASSACHUSETTS
WILLIAMS PAUL · SEAMAN 1C · USN · TENNESSEE
WILLIAMS ROBERT · SEAMAN 1C · USN · PENNSYLVANIA
TUCKER WILLIAM H · SEAMAN 1C · USN · CALIFORNIA
· PENNSYLVANIA

WILSON MORRIS H · SEAMAN 1C · USNR ·
WILSON OWEN FRANKLIN · SEAMAN 1C · USN ·
WILSON VINCENT · SEAMAN 1C · USN ·
WILSON WILLIAM E · CHIEF MACHINIST'S MATE ·
WILT JUNIOR DANIEL · GUNNER'S MATE 3C · U
WINDFELDT ALVIN L · SHIP'S COOK 1C · U
WING ARTHUR RAY · STOREKEEPER 2C · USN
WINIKA WALTER W · LIEUTENANT (JG) · USN
WINSLOW WARREN · LIEUTENANT · USNR
WINSTANLEY WILLIAM D · MACHINIST'S MATE 1C · U
WINTJEN GERALD C · SEAMAN 2C · U
WISER WILLIAM C · SEAMAN 1C · USN
WISHARD RAYMOND B · ENSIGN · USN
WISMER JOHN · SEAMAN 1C · USNR
WITHAM WILFRED R · SEAMAN 1C · USNR
WLODKOWSKI FRANCIS · SEAMAN 1C · US
WOLCHOK WILLIAM F · GUNNER'S MATE 3C · US
WOLFF JUSTIN L · LIEUTENANT (JG) · USNR
WOLFORD VINCENT A · MACHINIST'S MATE 3C · USN
WOLOSIN JOHN · SEAMAN 2C · USN
WOOD ALWYNNE W · CARPENTER'S MATE 2C · USN
WOOD ANDREW E · LIEUTENANT (JG) · USNR
WOOD ERNEST C · MOTOR MACHINIST'S MATE 2C
WOOD FRANK LEE · SEAMAN 1C · USN
WOODHULL ROBERT C · MACHINIST'S MATE 2C · USN
WOODS RALPH W · MACHINIST'S MATE 2C · USN
WOODS ROBERT L · SHIP'S COOK 1C · USN
WOODSIDE JOE L · SHIP'S COOK 1C · USN
WOODWARD LYMAN JR · METALSMITH 2C · USN
WOOL MEYER T · APPRENTICE SEAMAN · USNR
WOOLSEY WILLIAM J · SEAMAN 1C · USNR
WOOTEN CAREY LAVON · SEAMAN 1C · USN
WOOTTON RICHARD W · SEAMAN 1C · US
WORKMAN EDWARD JAMES · MACHINIST'S MATE 2C
WORRELL GERALD T · AVN RADIOMAN 2C
WOSINSKI AELRED Q · SIGNALMAN 3C · USN
WRANEK ALBERT R · SEAMAN 1C · USNR
WRIGHT CHARLES D · ENSIGN · USNR
WRIGHT ROBERT ALLEN · TORPEDOMAN'S MATE 1C
WRIGHT STANLEY JR · SEAMAN 2C · USNR
WRIGHT WALTER E · MACHINIST'S MATE 2C · U
WRIGHT WILLIAM W · MOTOR MACH MATE 3C
WRONSKI EDWARD F · SEAMAN 1C · USN
WULTHORST CARL A · APPRENTICE SEAMAN · US
WYATT HARRY E JR · APPRENTICE SEAMAN ·
WYDEEN WALLACE A · LIEUTENANT (JG) · USN
WYGANT HENRY S JR · COMMANDER · USN
WYLDER DONALD LEE · SEAMAN 1C · US
WYLIE HOWARD EUGENE · APPRENTICE SEAMAN
WYNN JOHN HARMON · APPRENTICE SEAMAN ·
YAFFE IRVING HERMAN · SEAMAN 1C · USN
YANNELLA LOUIS · APPRENTICE SEAMAN · US
YARMAT HARRY A · SEAMAN 2C · USN
YAROSCZAK MICHAEL · SEAMAN 2C · USNR
YATES FRANCIS D · APPRENTICE SEAMAN ·
YAW ROBERT L · AVN ORDNANCEMAN 3C · US
YODICE GENARO J · SEAMAN 1C · USNR
YOST RICHARD J · SEAMAN 1C · USNR
YOUNG ALFRED HORACE · SEAMAN 1C · US
YOUNG CARROLL T · RADIOMAN 2C · USNR
YOUNG EARLE E · MACHINIST'S MATE 2C · USNR
YOUNG JAMES R · AVN MACHINIST'S MATE 2C · U
YOUNG RICHARD J · ELECTRICIAN'S MATE 2C · US
YOUNG WILLIE DANIEL · STEWARD'S MATE 2C · U
ZACHARIAS CASPER · LIEUTENANT · USNR
ZACK EUGENE G · SEAMAN 1C ·
ZAIONTZ JOSEPH PETER · COXSWAIN ·
ZAJKOWSKY BENJAMIN · FIREMAN 1C · US
ZAMIATOWSKI JEROME A · SEAMAN 2C · USN
ZAMUNER ENZO BRUNO · SEAMAN 2C · US
ZARELLI ANTONIO J · RADIO TECHNICIAN 2C · U
ZAYDELL WALTER J · RADIOMAN 3C · U
ZEBROWSKI EDWARD F · APPRENTICE SEAMAN ·
ZEIDLER CARL E · LIEUTENANT (JG) · USNR
ZEIGER JOSEPH M · BOATSWAIN'S MATE 2C · U
ZERINGUE PHILIP J · MACHINIST'S MATE 1C · US
ZEROZ LEO VINCENT · SEAMAN 1C · US
ZIMMERMAN JOHN W · SEAMAN 2C · USN
ZIMMERMANN GEORGE A · FIREMAN 3C · USN
ZINK OSWALD A · LIEUTENANT (JG) · USN
ZINN EDWARD A · SEAMAN 2C · USN
ZION JOSEPH · AVN RADIO TECHNICIAN 1C · U
ZOLLER RUSSELL A · YEOMAN 3C · US
ZUKIEWICZ GEORGE J · AVN ORDNANCEMAN 3C · U
ZYLA MICHAEL N · SEAMAN 1C · USNR
AMERICAN BATTLE
MONUMENTS COMMISSION

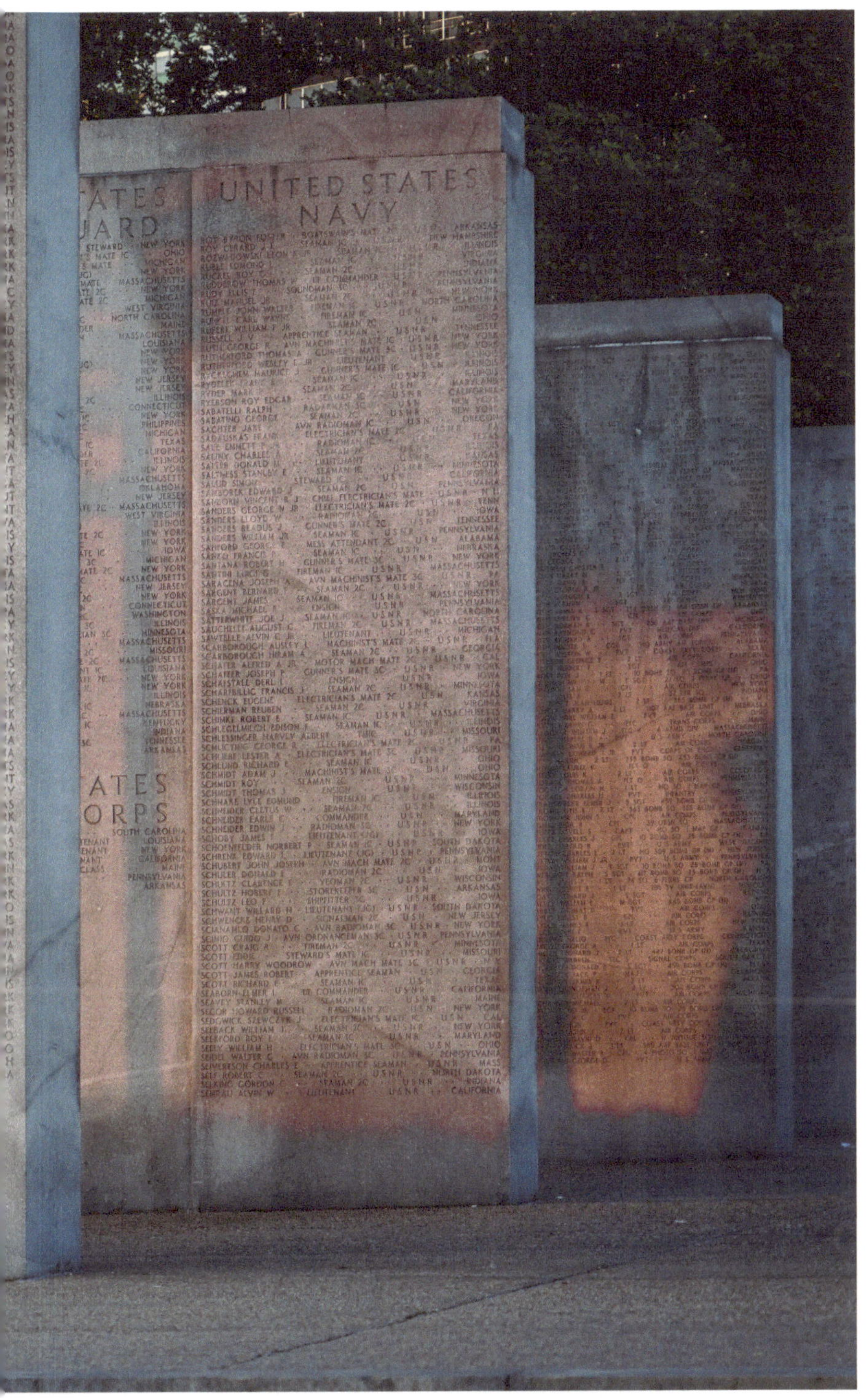

She waits in the fading light, holding a silence no monument can answer.

CH 5 . BETWEEN US, THE CITY

Between every passerby and every towering façade
lies a distance the city never explains.

Some days, it draws us closer,
folding our stories into its lights;
other days, it keeps its distance,
reminding us that intimacy here is always fleeting.

In these images, the city becomes a third presence—
a witness, a barrier,
and a translator of emotions we cannot name.

What stands between us is not emptiness,
but the city's gentle yet stubborn pulse—
sometimes pulling us together,
sometimes quietly letting us drift apart.

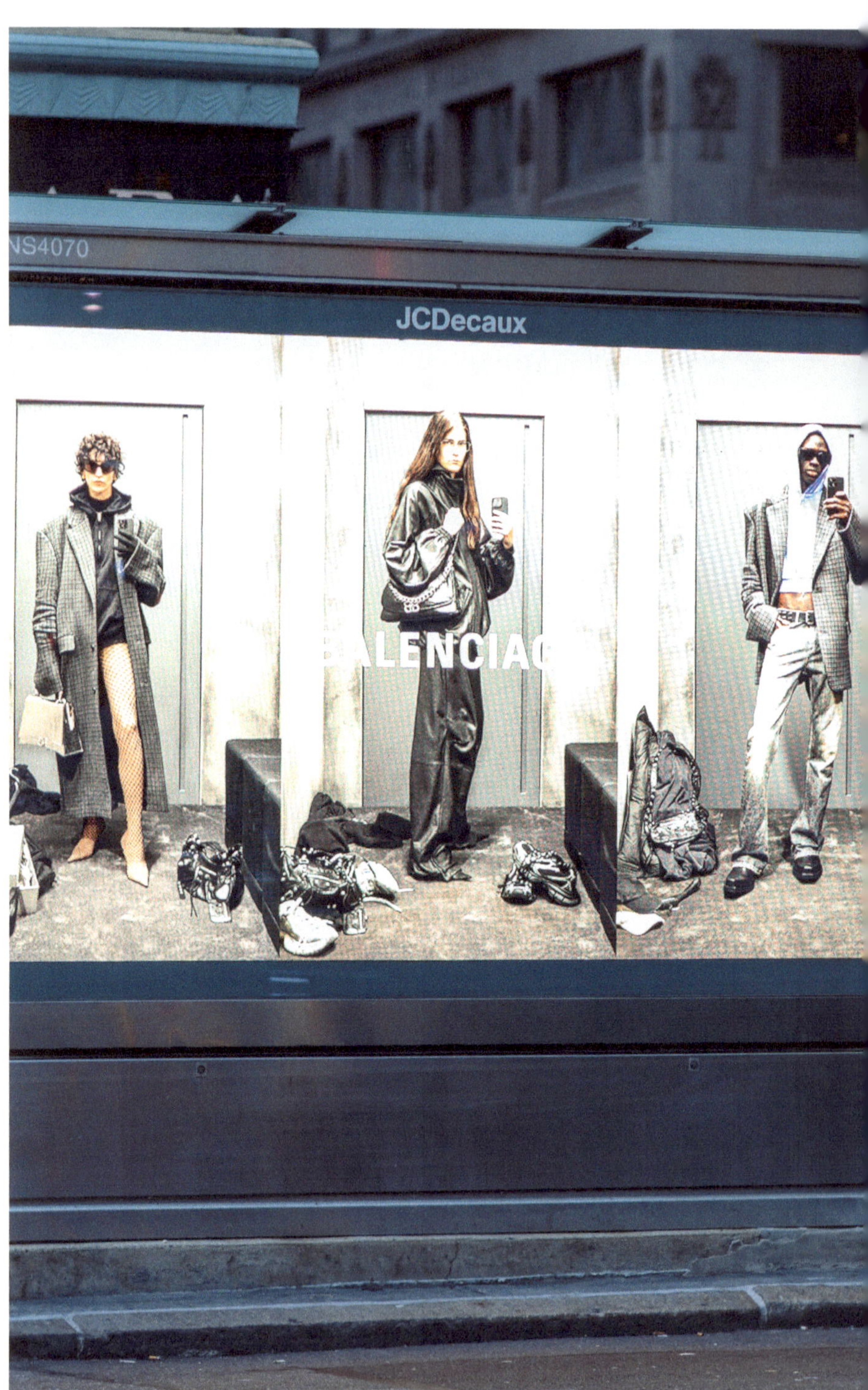
NS4070
JCDecaux
BALENCIAGA

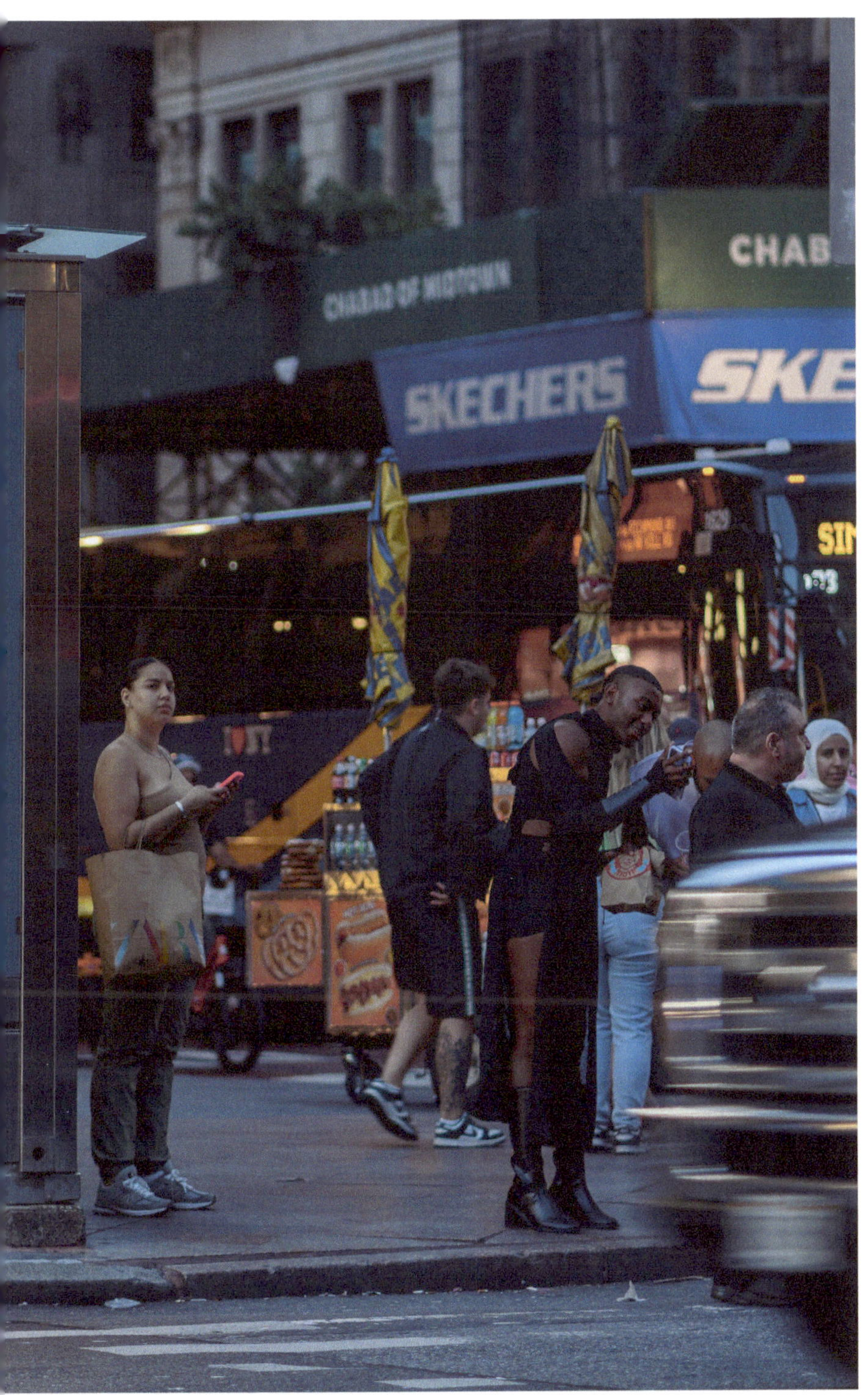

Between who we are and who we pretend to be lies the real city.

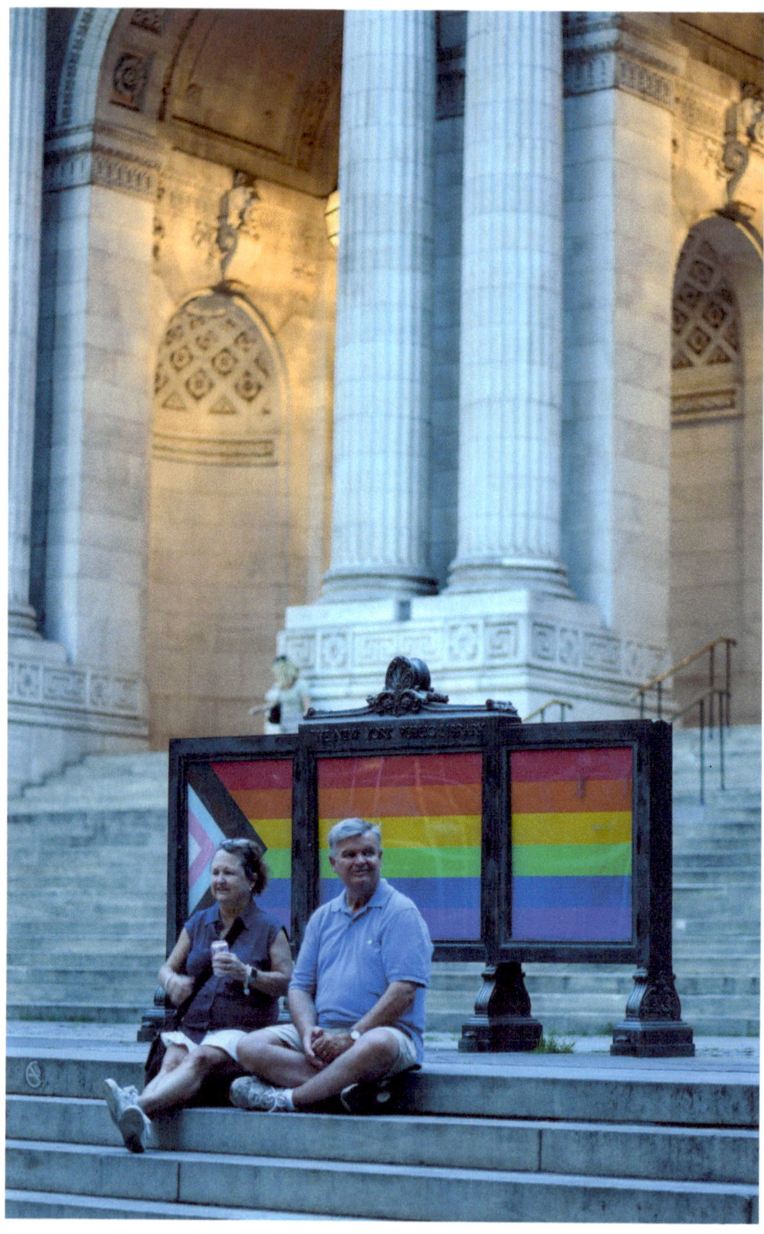

Sometimes two people create their own quiet nation.

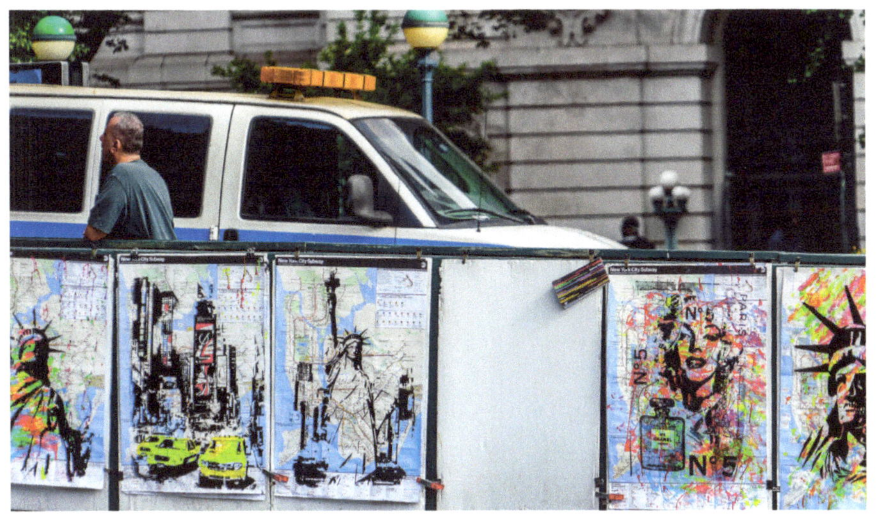

Art blooms where the city forgets to look.

He lifts his phone like a quiet prayer , hoping the moment will bless him back.

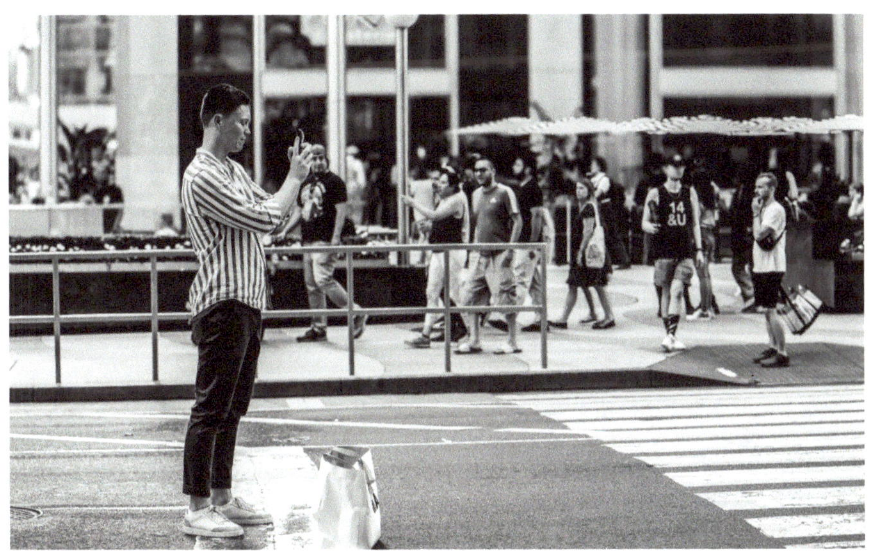

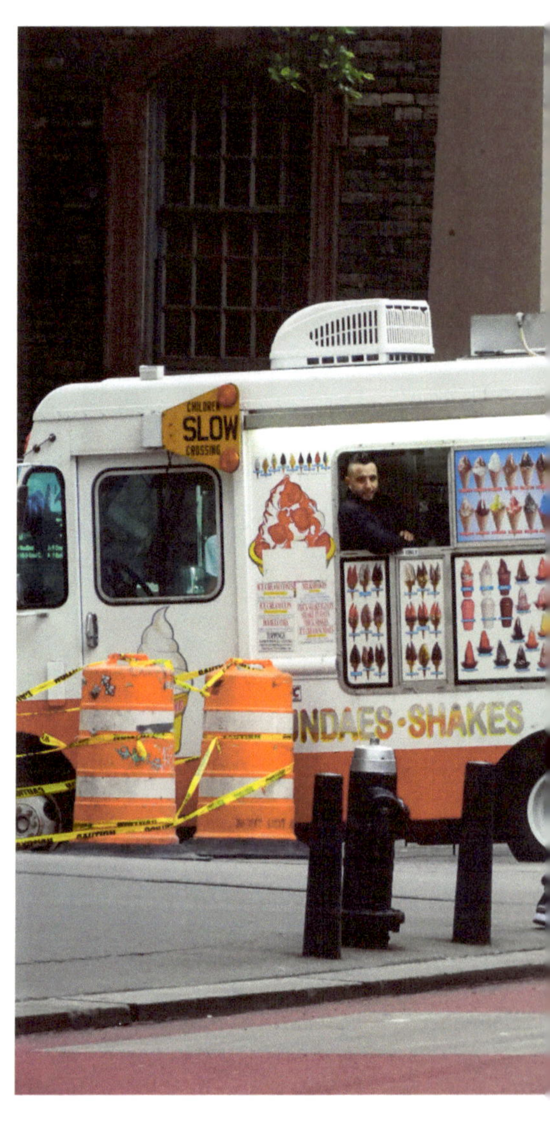

Unsure who listens—yet certain the city needs the sound.

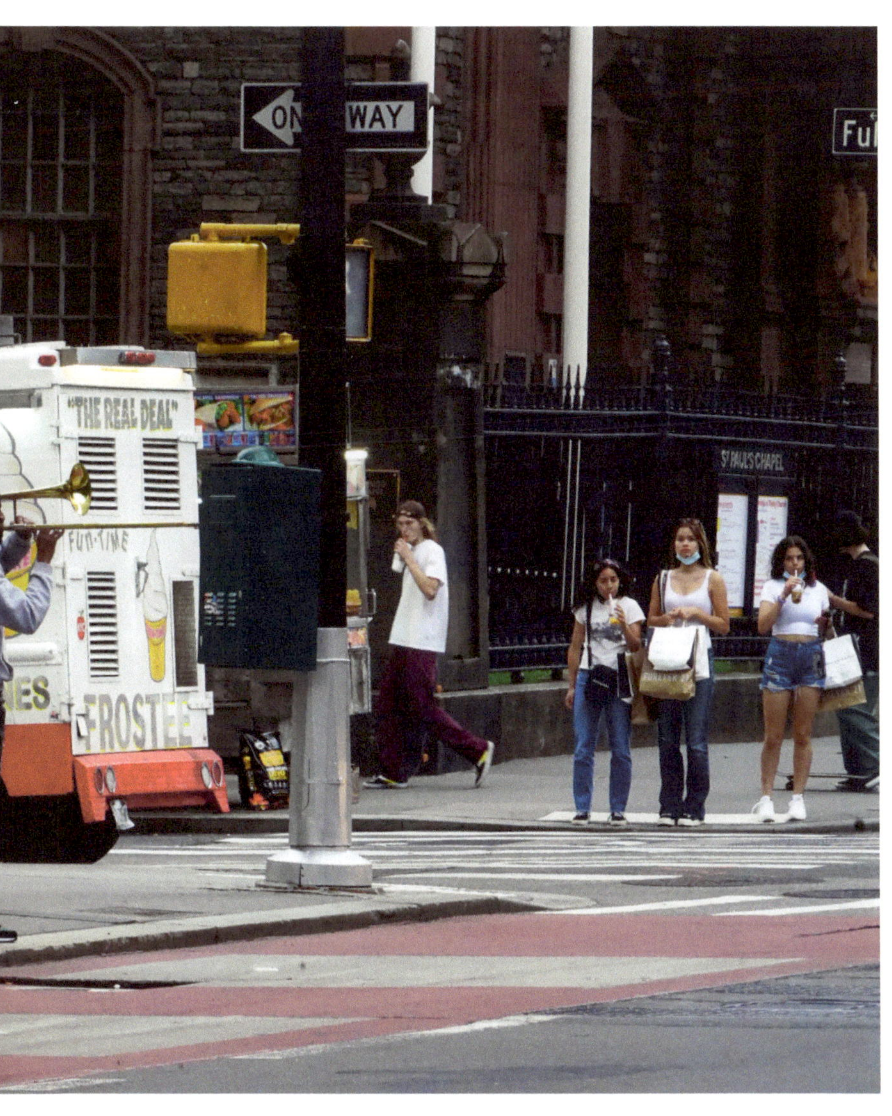

ONE WAY
Fu
"THE REAL DEAL"
FUN-TIME
FROSTEE
S! PAUL'S CHAPEL

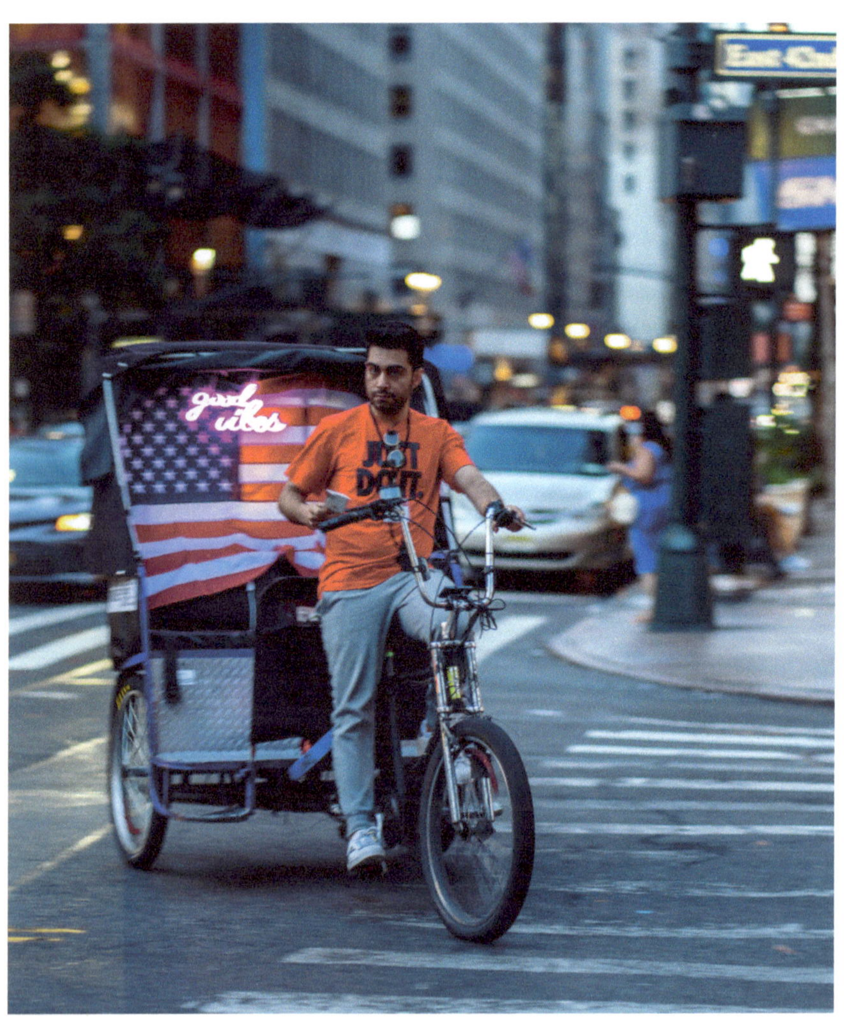

He threads the city like a pulse—steady, stubborn, defiantly alive.

He lifts his gaze with the tourists—yet only he pretends to know the city' s answers.

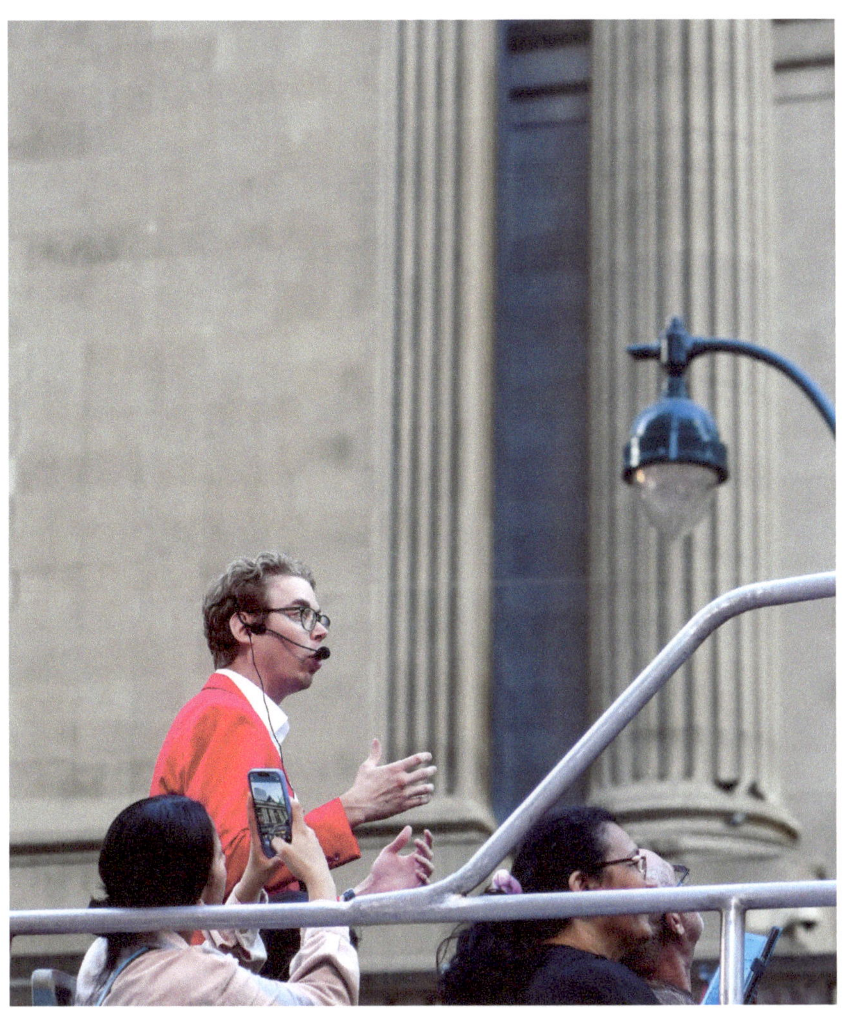

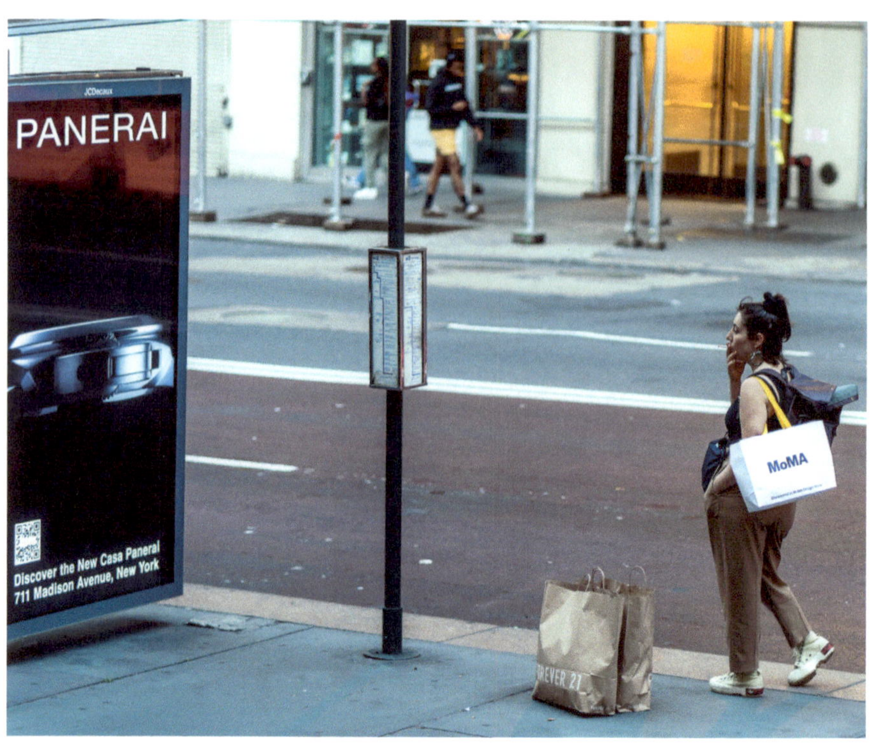

The city waits for her to choose what to carry.

Only coins, glances—a ritual the city repeats every day.

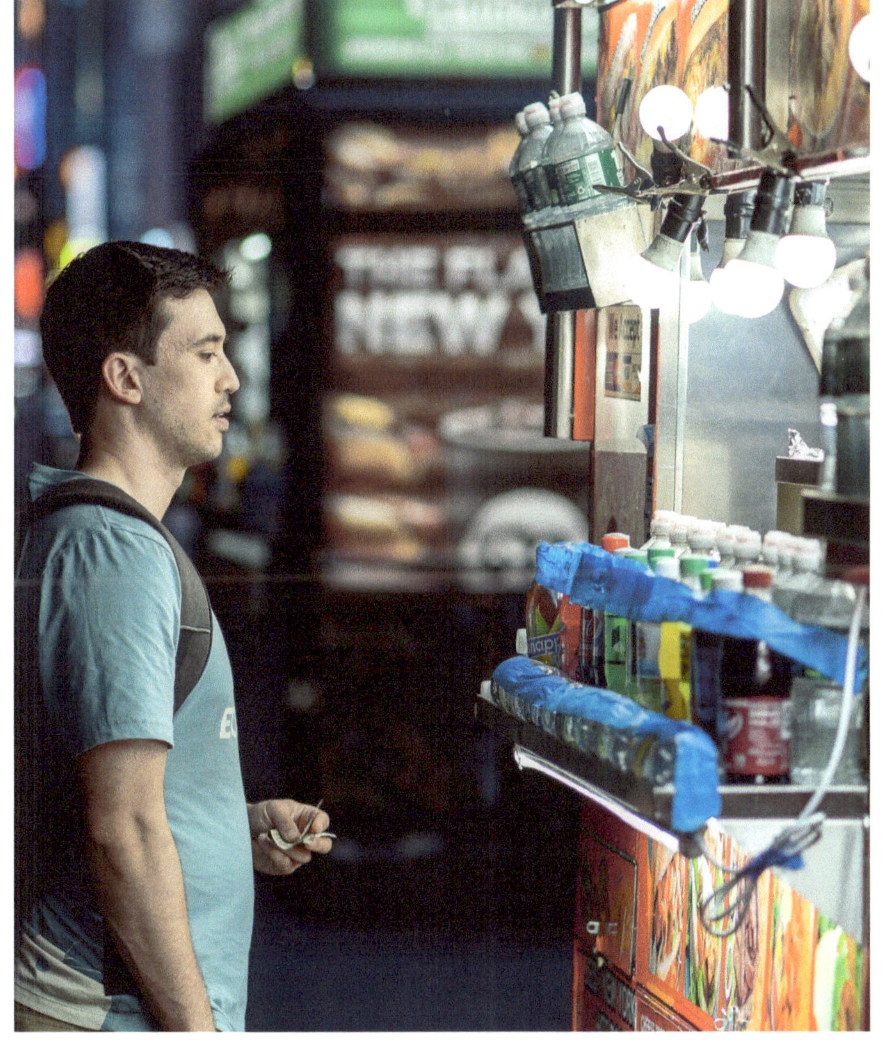

CH 6 . URBAN HUMOR & VITALITY

New York is never only serious.
Beneath the steel and speed, order and ambition,
the city keeps slipping in moments of absurd grace—
a flash of color out of place, a pigeon crossing against the light,
a dancer claiming the sidewalk as a stage.

The city looks chaotic, even indifferent, but it is deeply alive.
Its humor isn't polite and its warmth isn't performative.
New York doesn't ask who you are, and it doesn't pretend to care—
yet somehow, it makes room for everyone.

Billionaires and buskers, dreamers and the lost,
all move through the same streets without explanation.
The city neither flatters nor rejects.
It simply lets you exist.

And in that freedom—
life keeps finding ways to smile back.

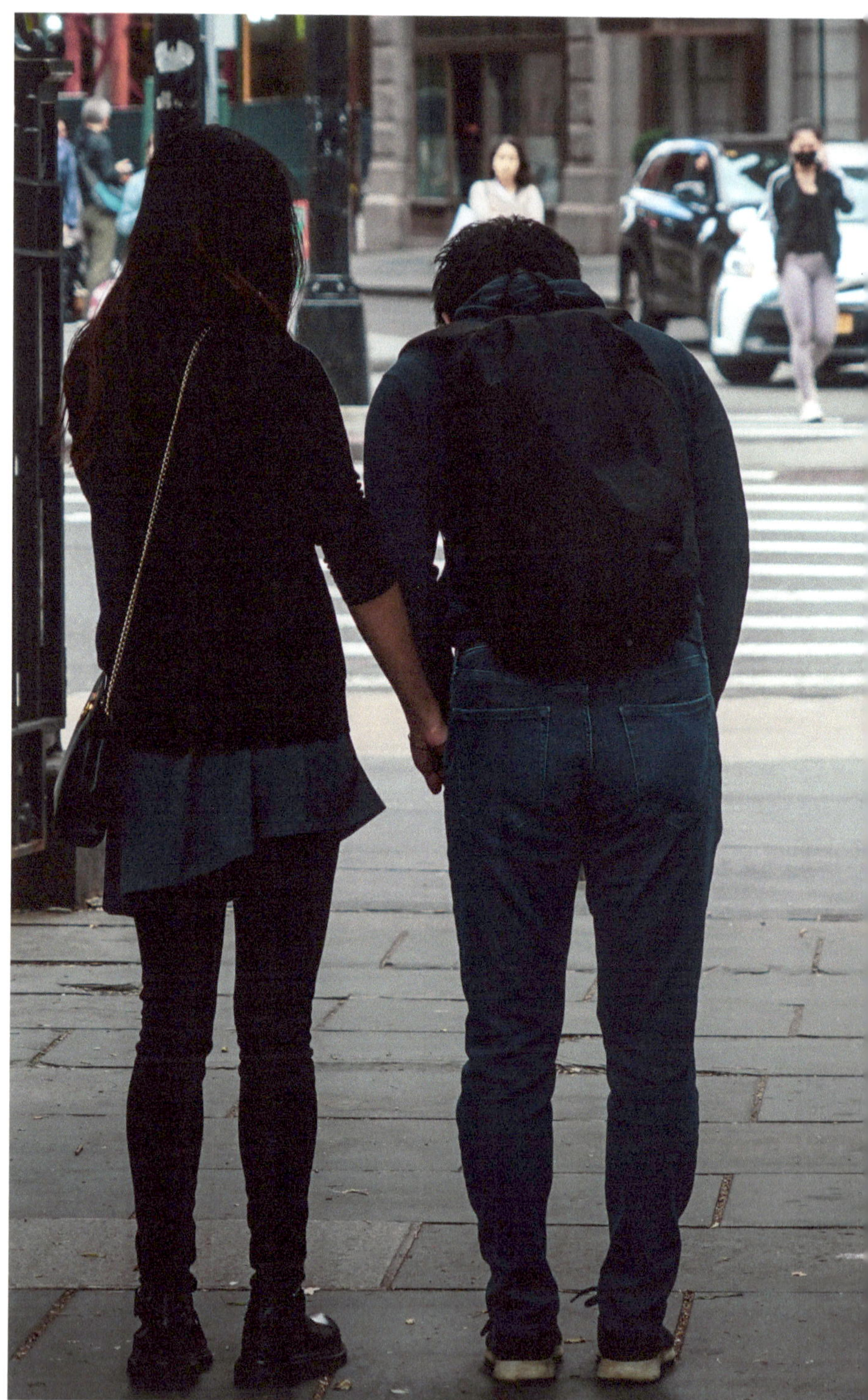

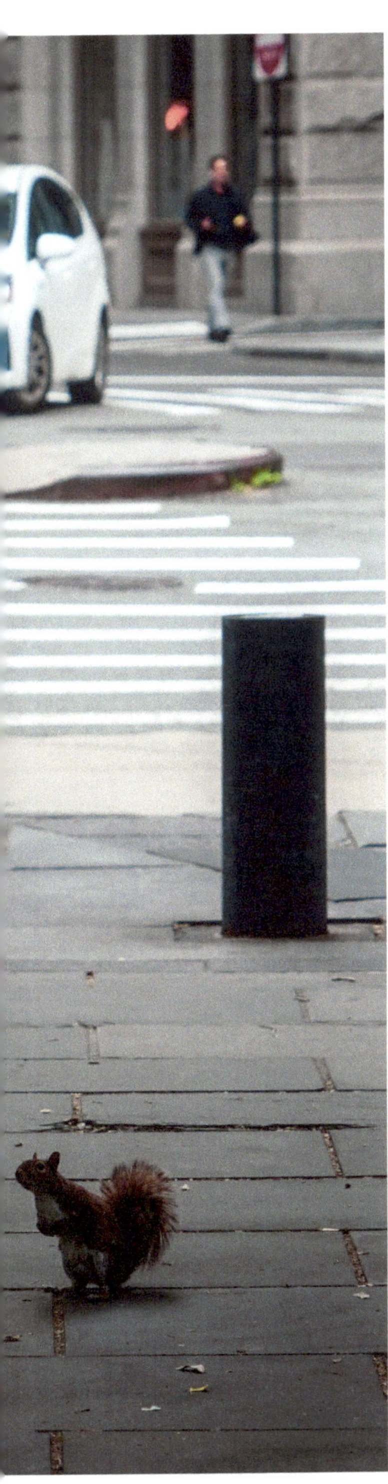

Love walks slowly here—
often because someone very small refuses to hurry.

The city may be heavy, but the boy always finds a lighter way to touch it.

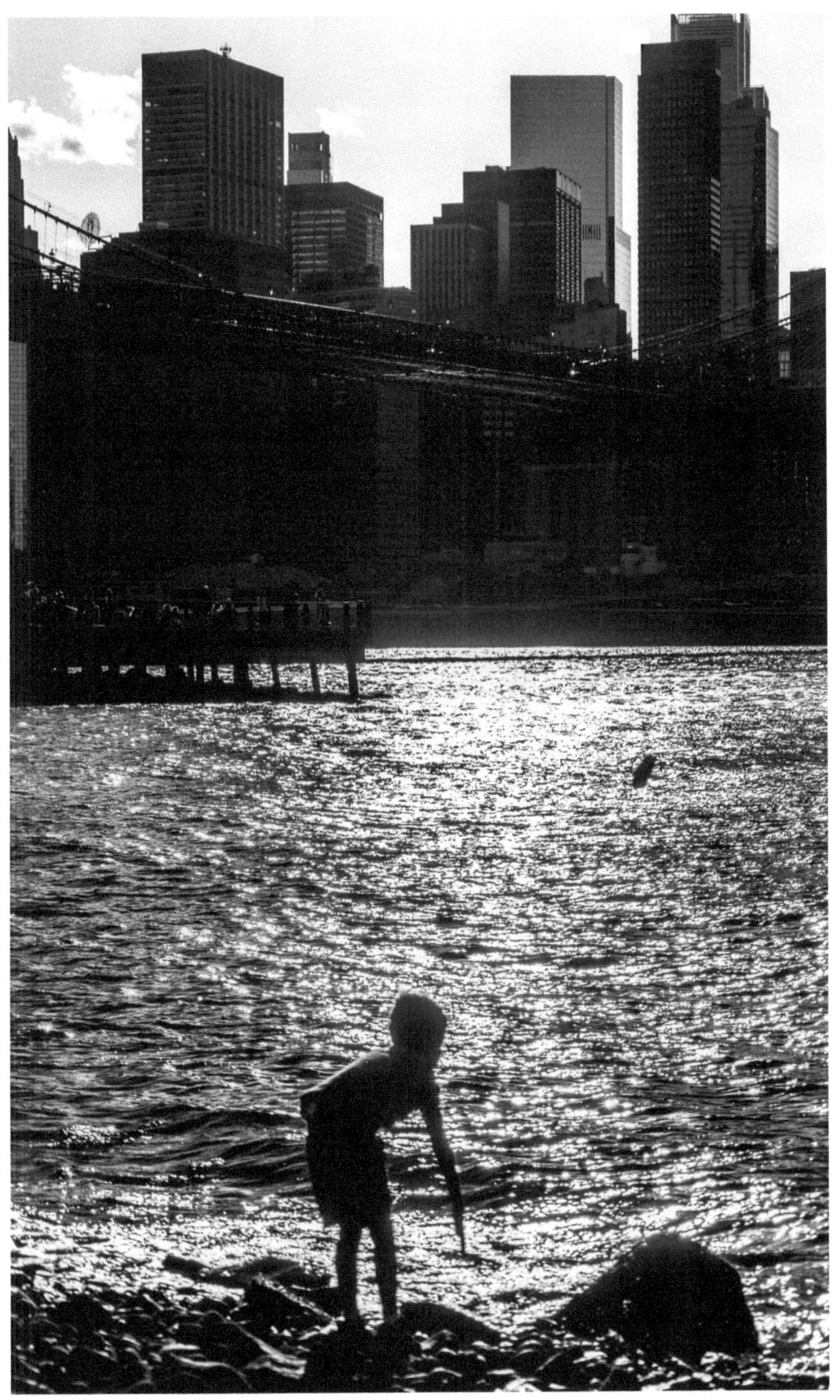

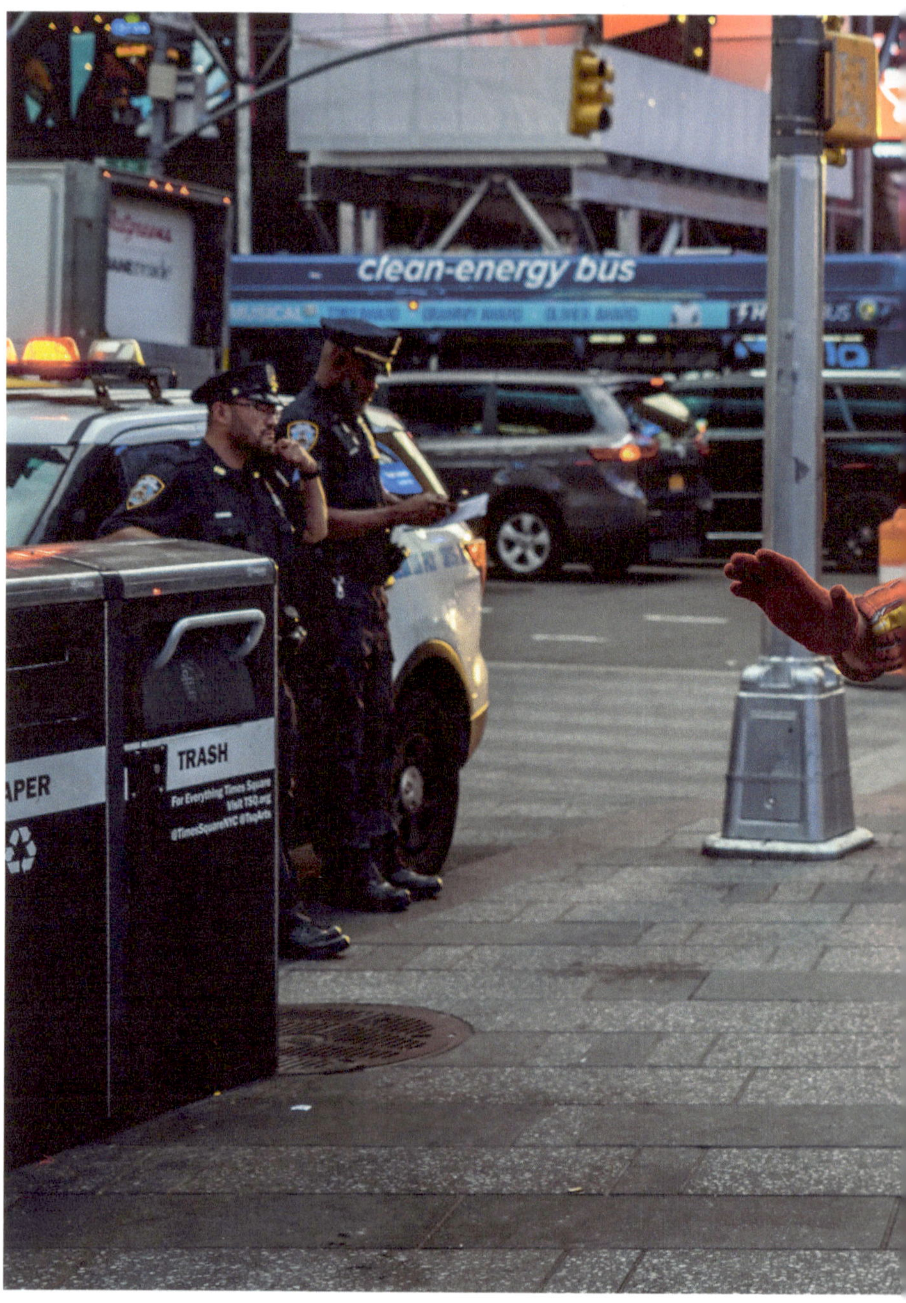
clean-energy bus
TRASH
For Everything Times Square
Visit TSQ.org
@TimesSquareNYC @TsqArts
PAPER

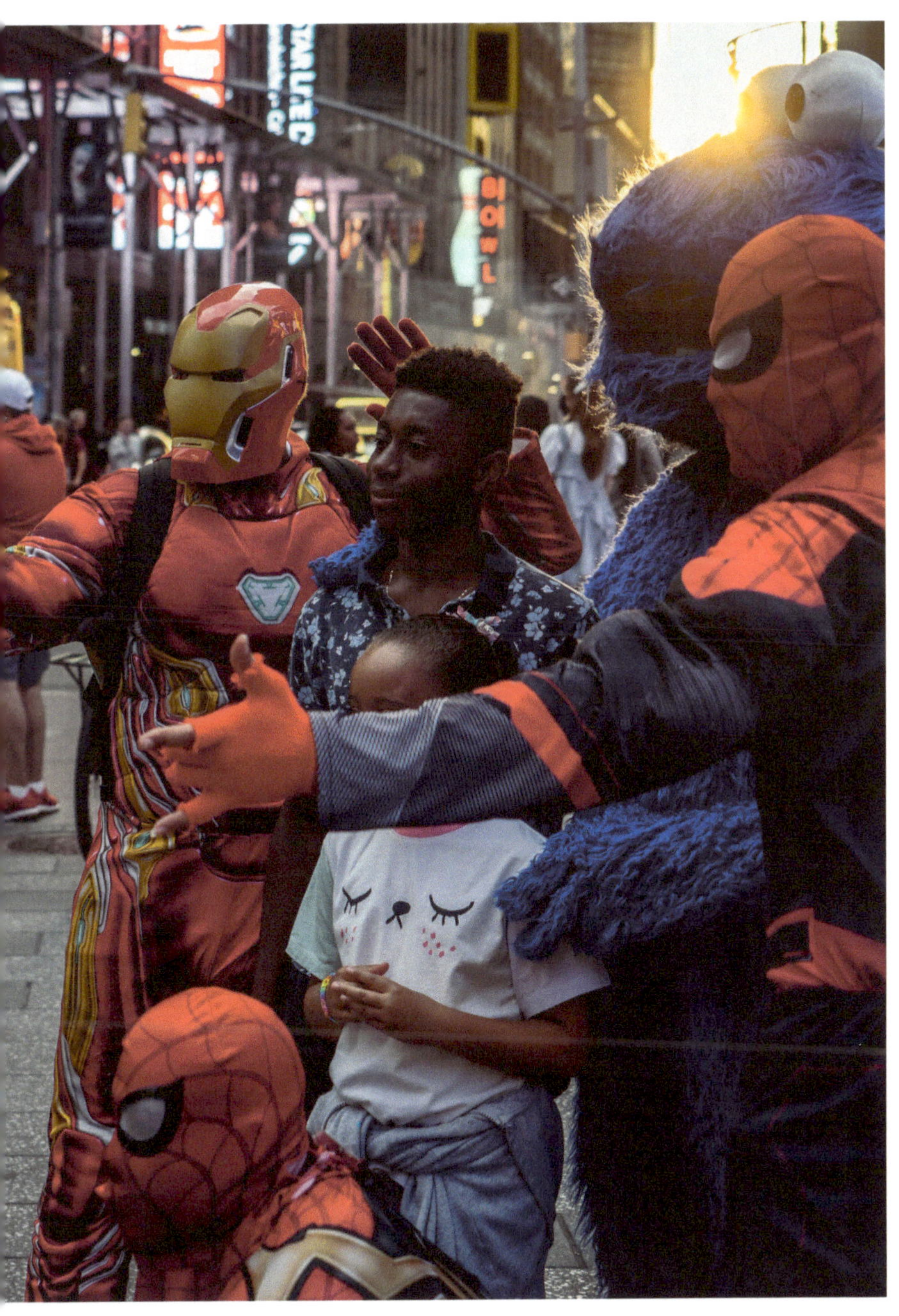

In New York, even heroes take shifts—and joy arrives on schedule.

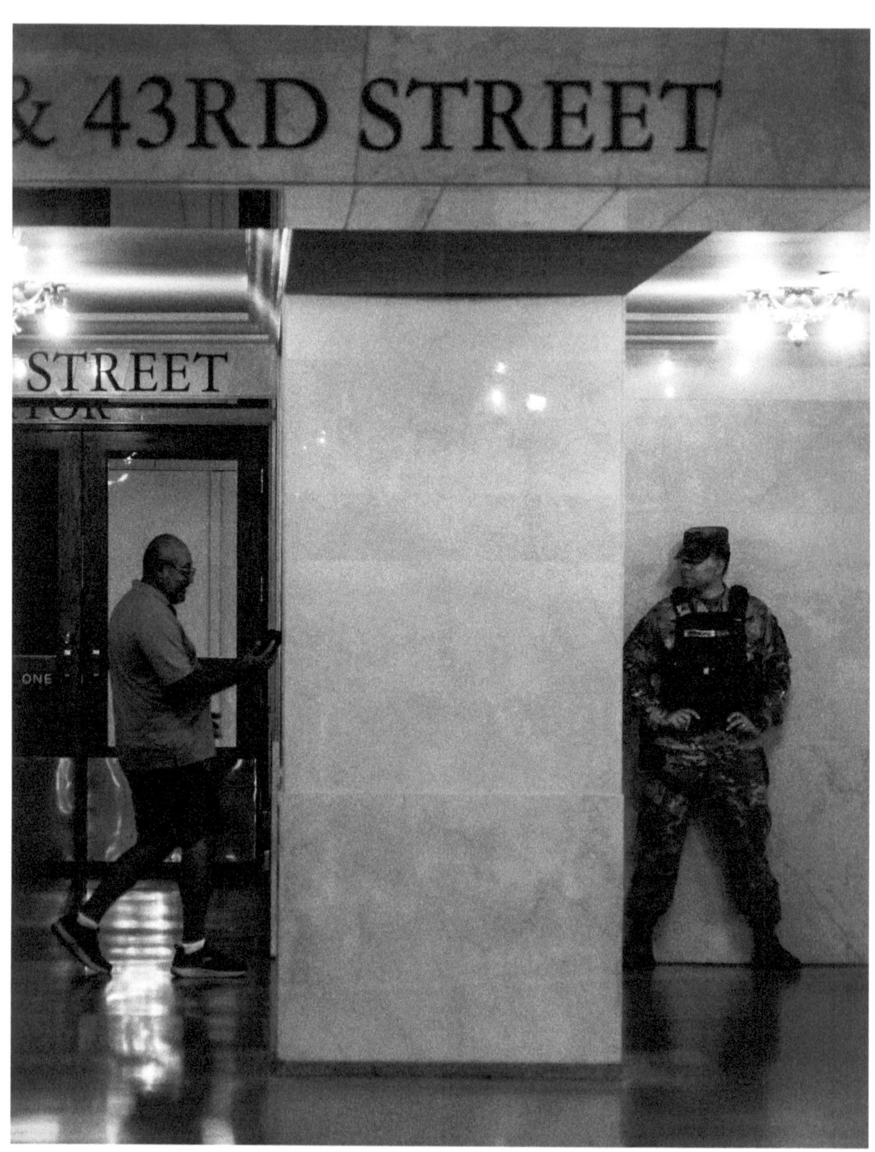

He's not only guarding a station — he' s guiding the lost through the noise.

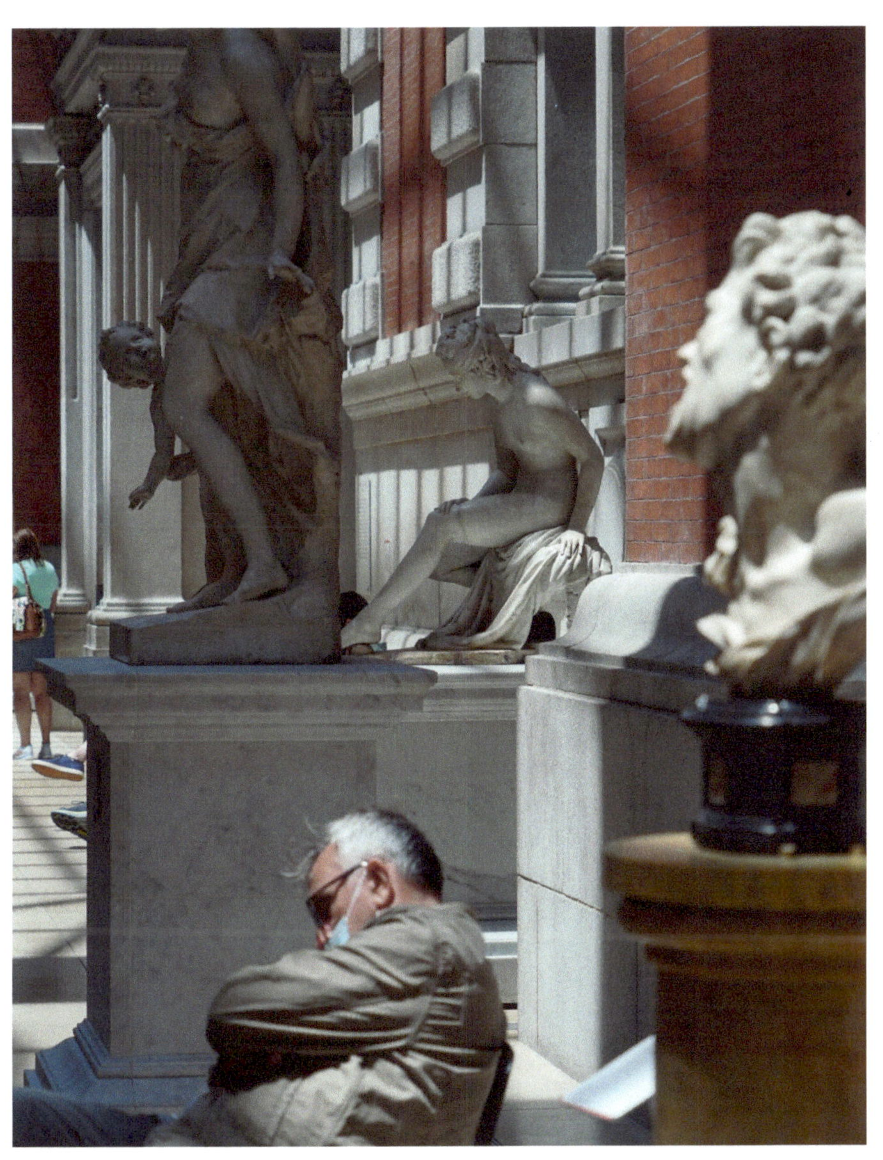

Even the gods don't mind sharing their silence with the tired.

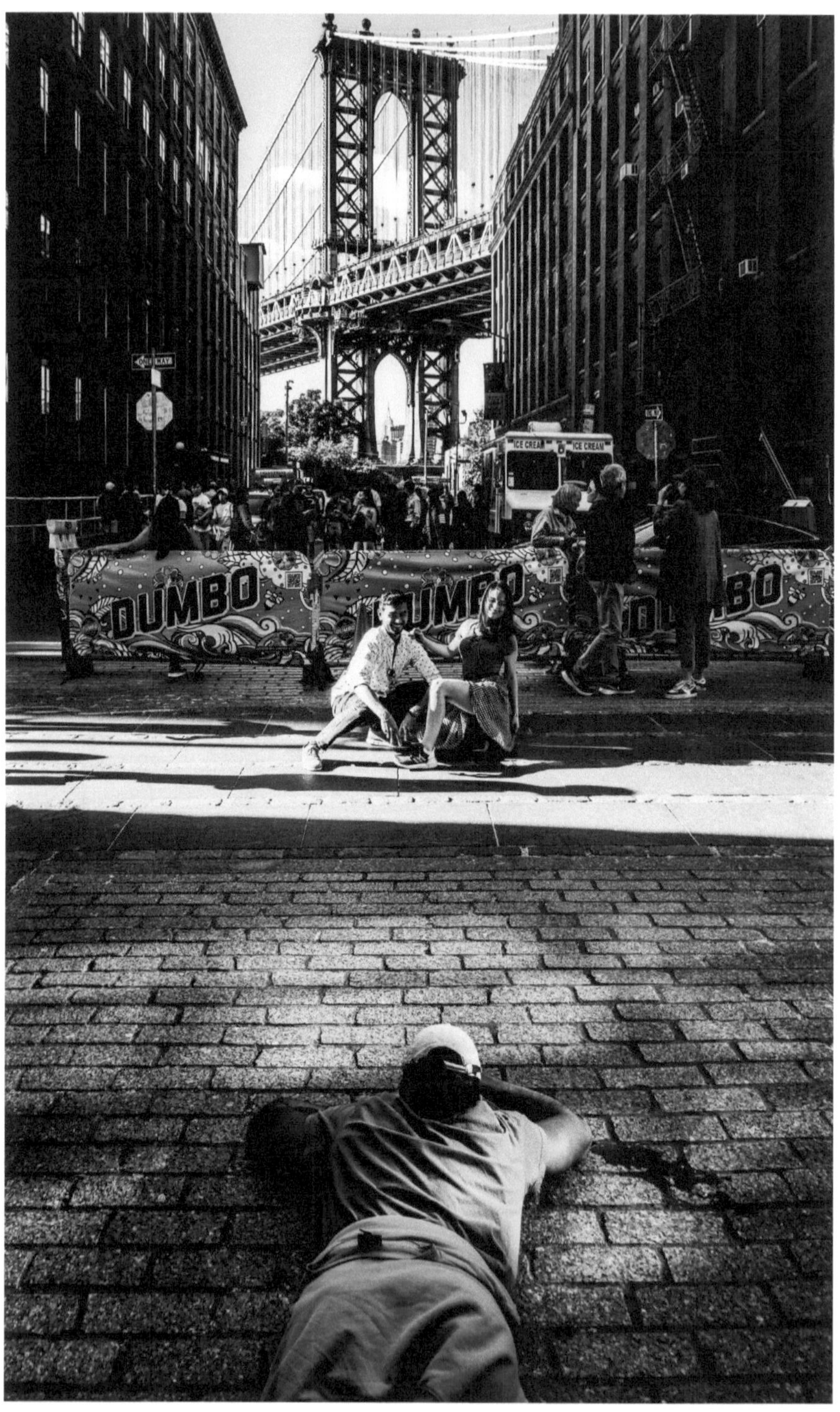
ONE WAY
DUMBO
DUMBO
DUMBO
ICE CREAM
ICE CREAM

To capture the perfect shot, dignity is often the first sacrifice.

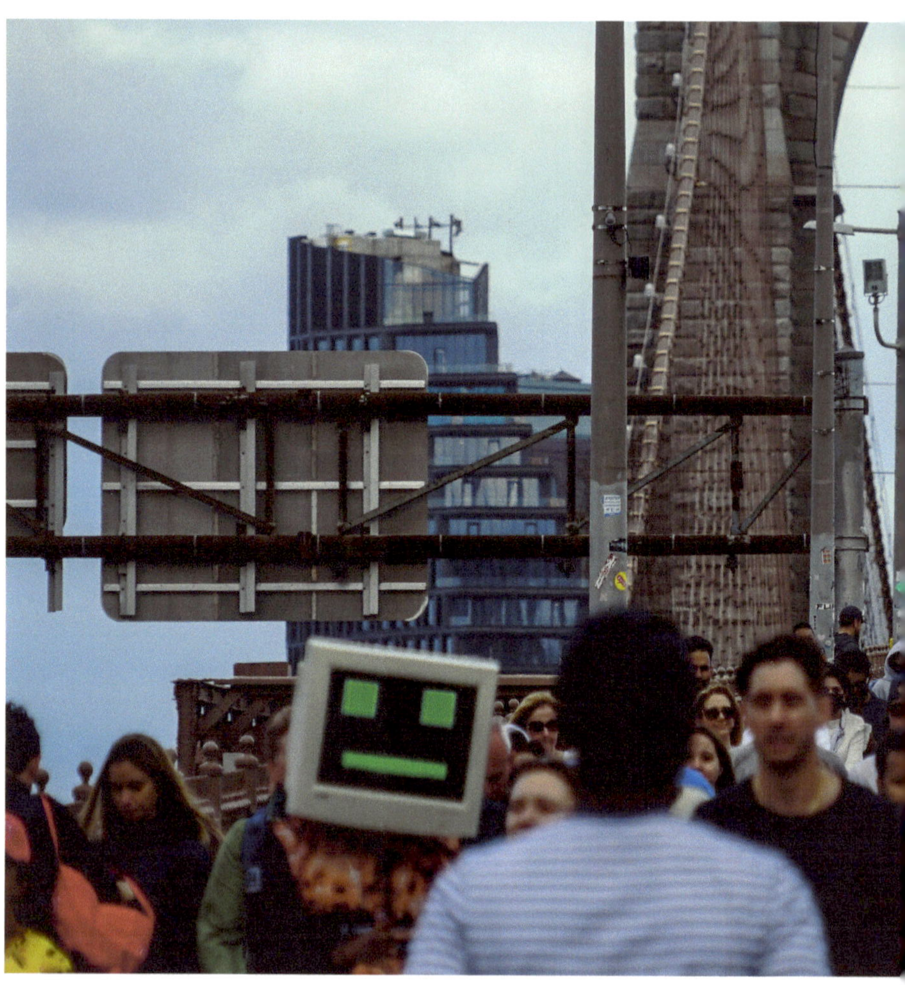

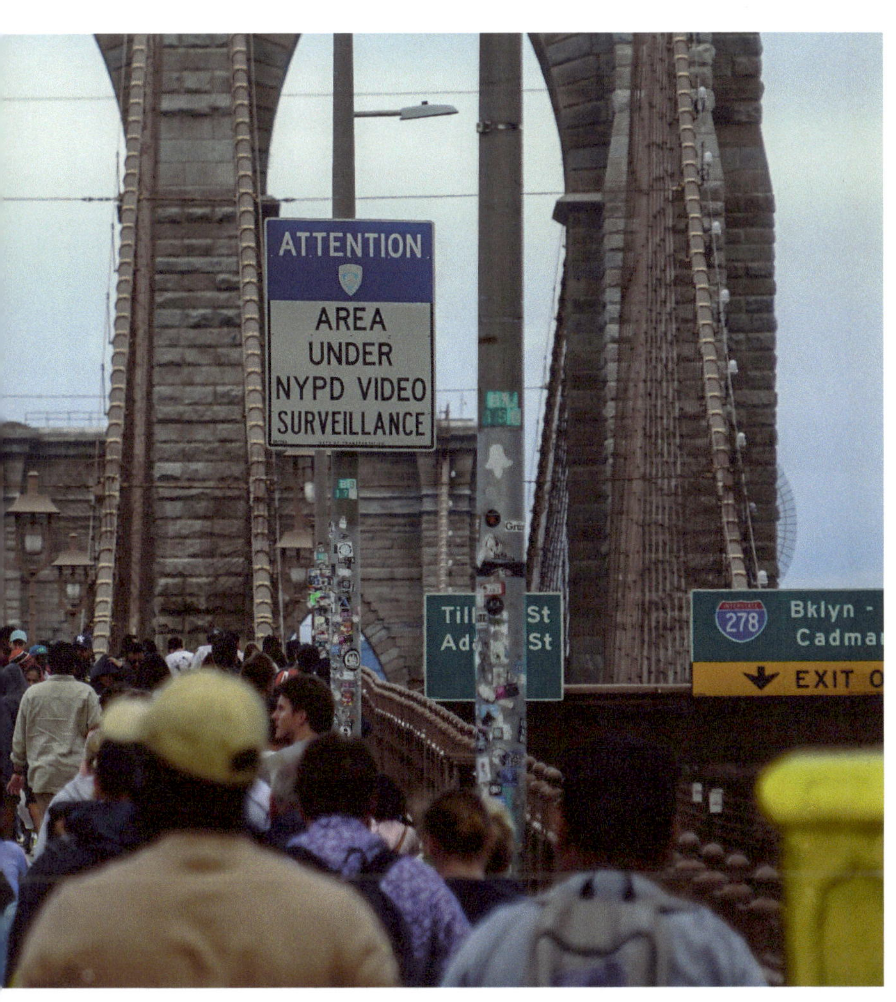

Everyone crosses the bridge; no one crosses it for the same reason.

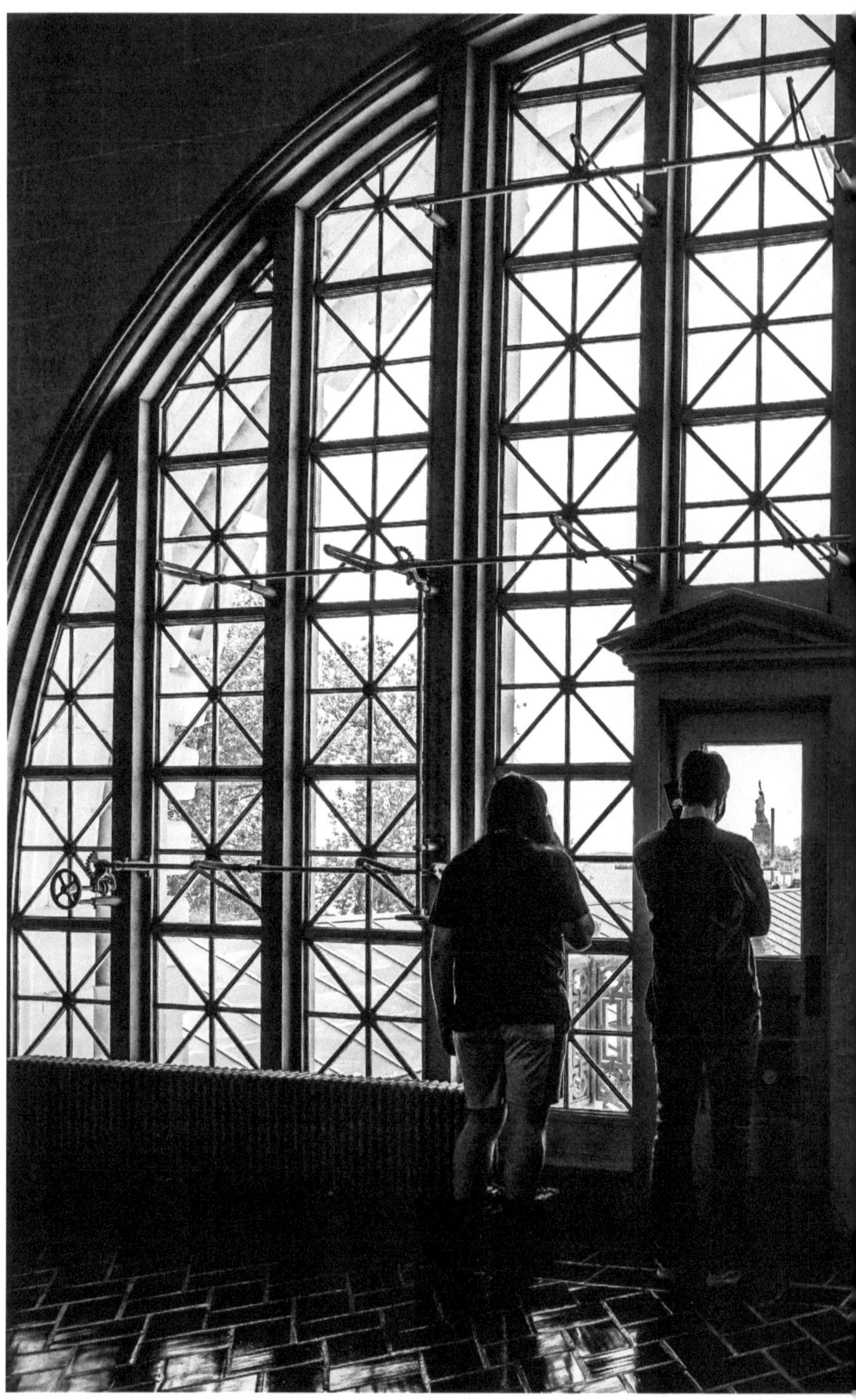

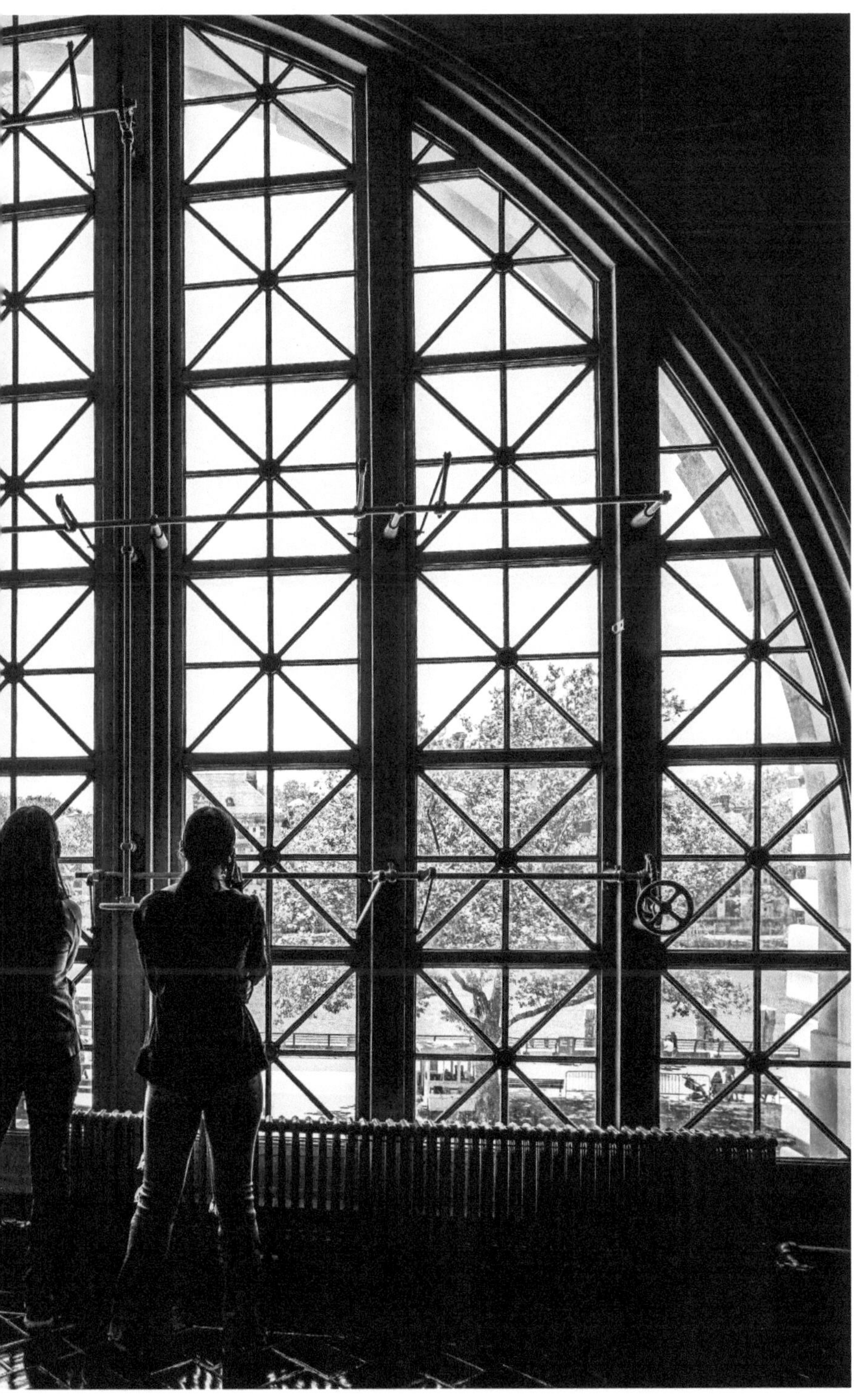

Briefly bound by the same beam of history , as if time had forgotten to separate them.

CH 7 . TWILIGHT OF STILL FIRE

Twilight in New York is never fully dark.
It glows—restrained, persistent—
like a secret the city refuses to surrender.

Noise softens into memory.
Footsteps dissolve into echoes.
Reflections turn inward.

Here, the city burns quietly:
in neon breathing like a pulse,
in windows holding a single figure,
in streets where loneliness and beauty
briefly speak the same language.

These photographs follow what lingers between day and night—
a light that asks for nothing,
only to be seen.

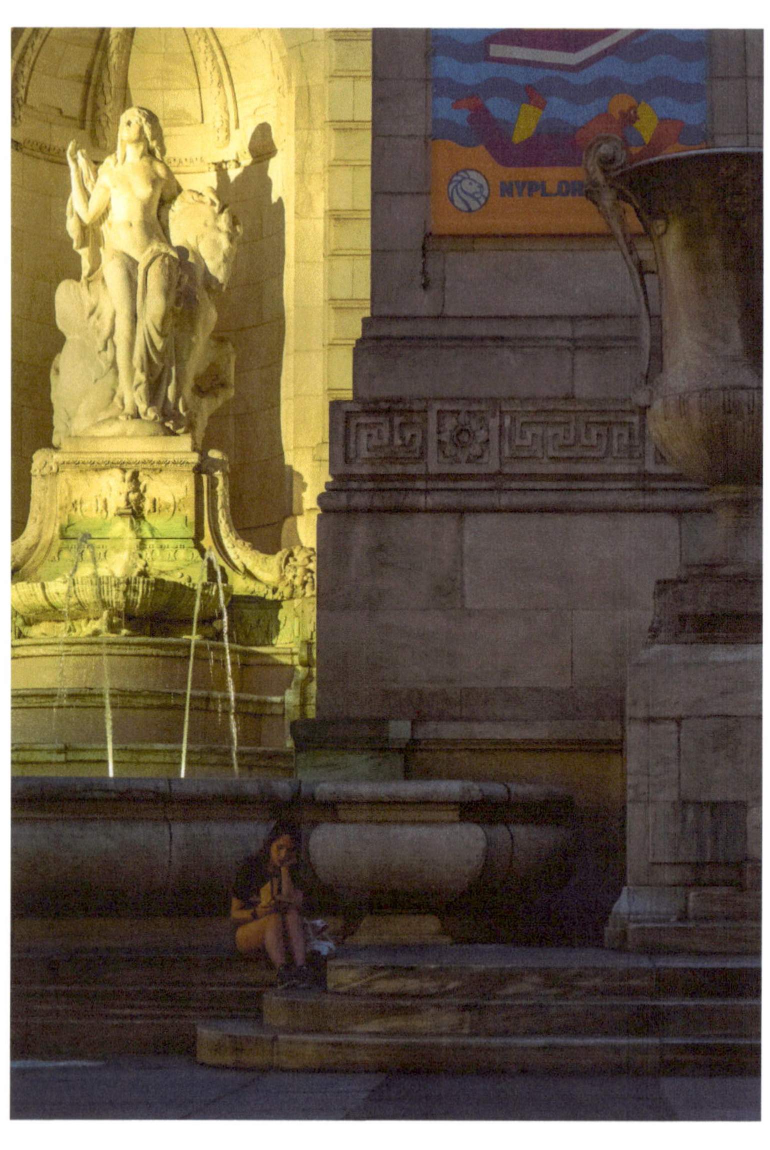

She keeps reading—a quiet witness to a story she hasn't yet entered.

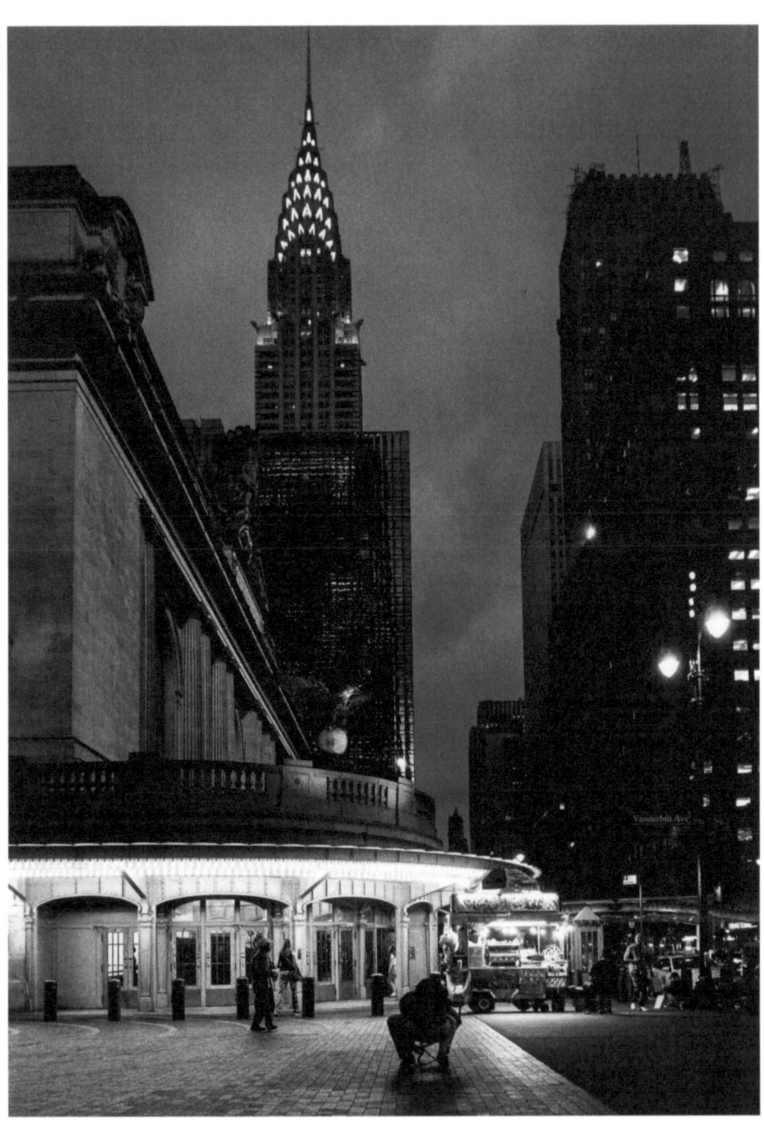

Under the pale glow, he frames the city; in the shadows, I frame him.

She waits—not at the center of the light,but where the night refuses to end.

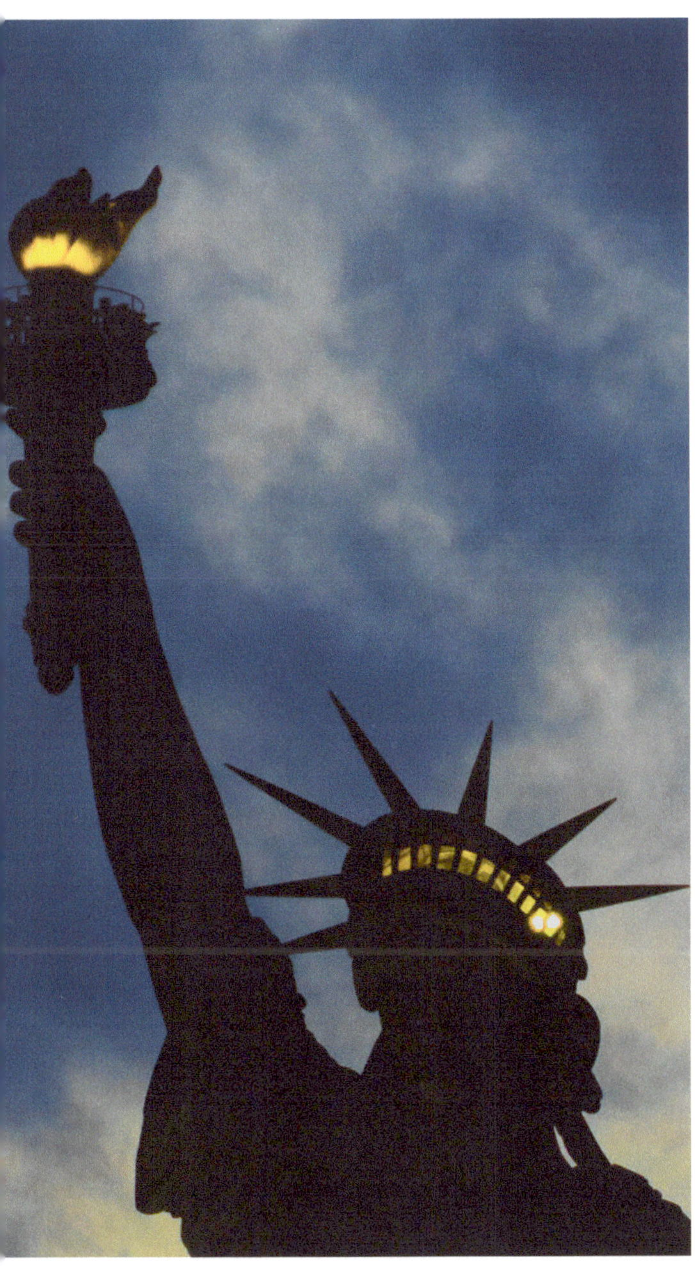

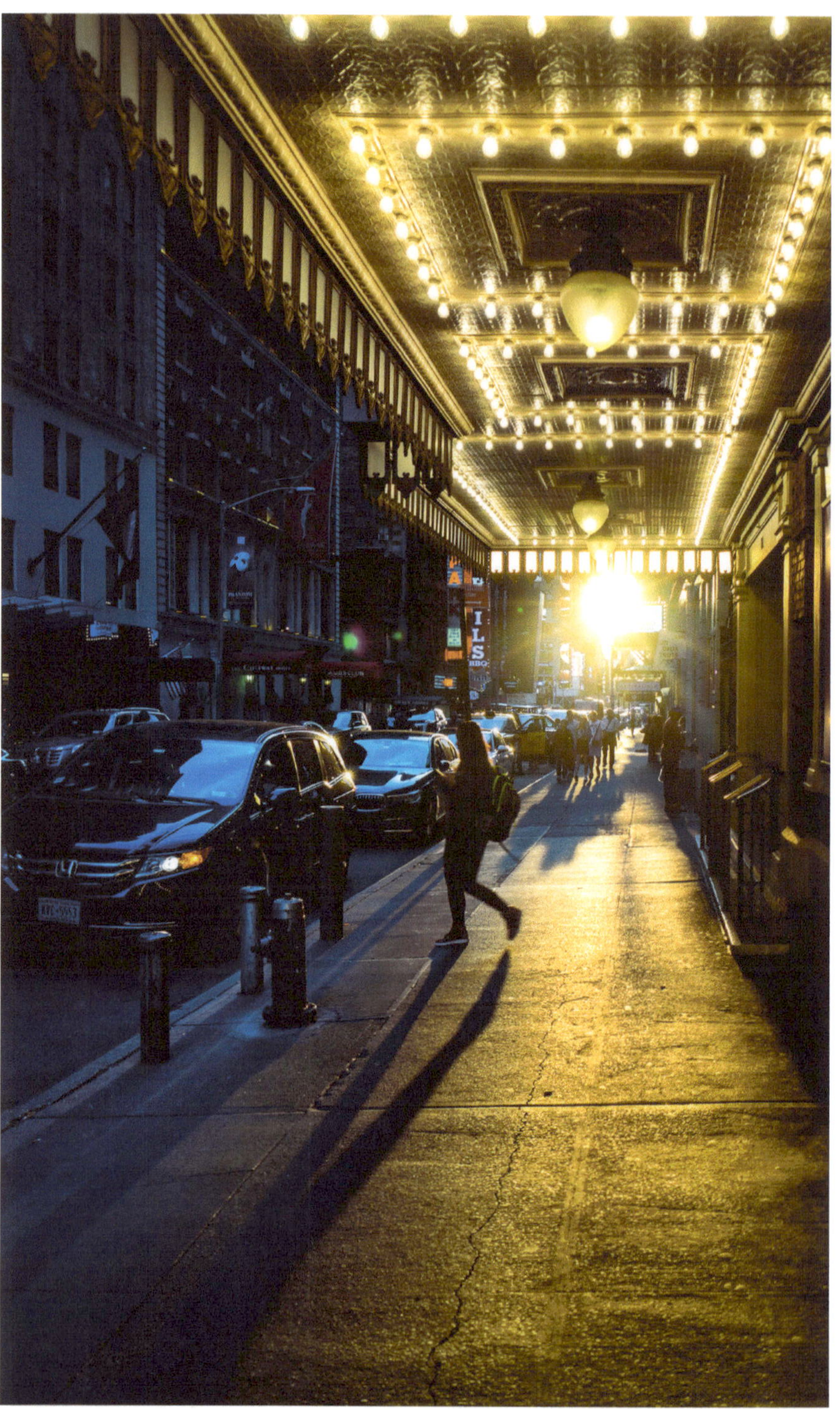

At the edge of Broadway, every shadow longs to become a story.

Trash bags beside ice cream—in NYC, the absurd and the iconic share the same sidewalk.

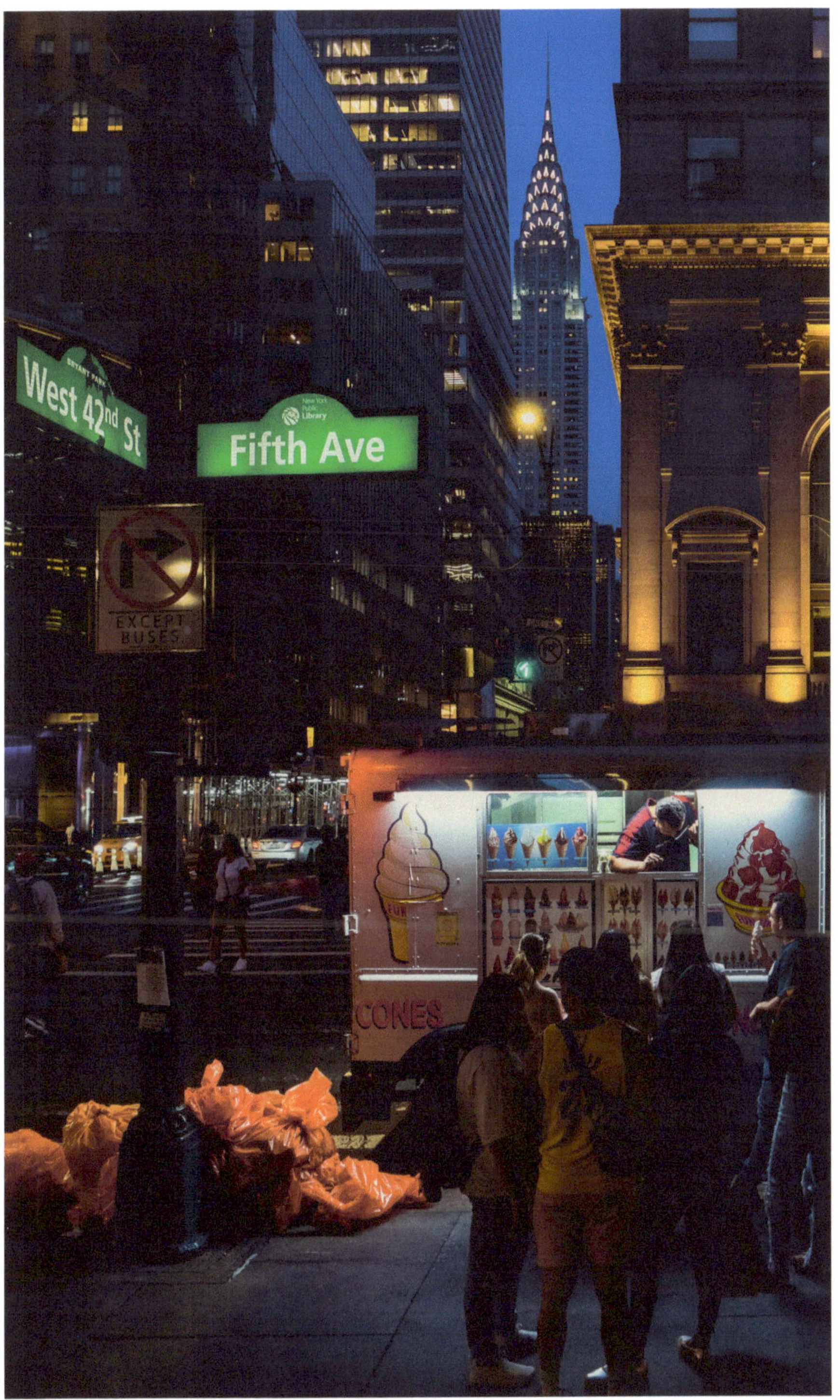
West 42nd St
New York Public Library
Fifth Ave
EXCEPT BUSES
CONES

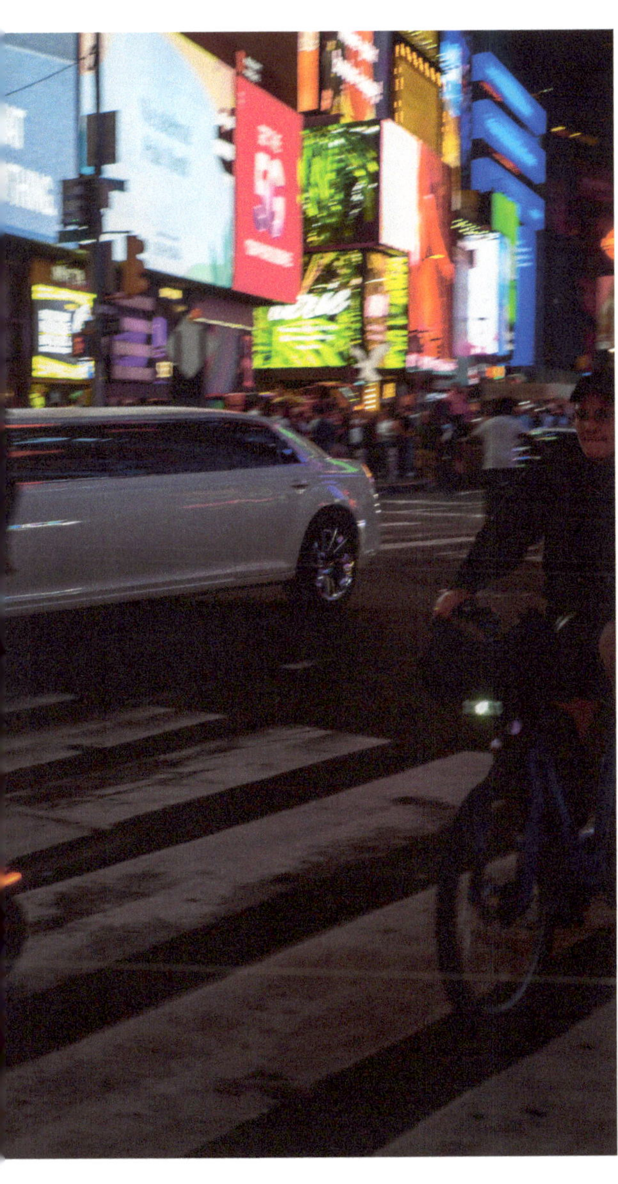

Each glide signs an unspoken pact—youth borrowing a piece of the night's infinite dark.

He watches the crowd glow—not yet part of the night,not ready to leave the day.

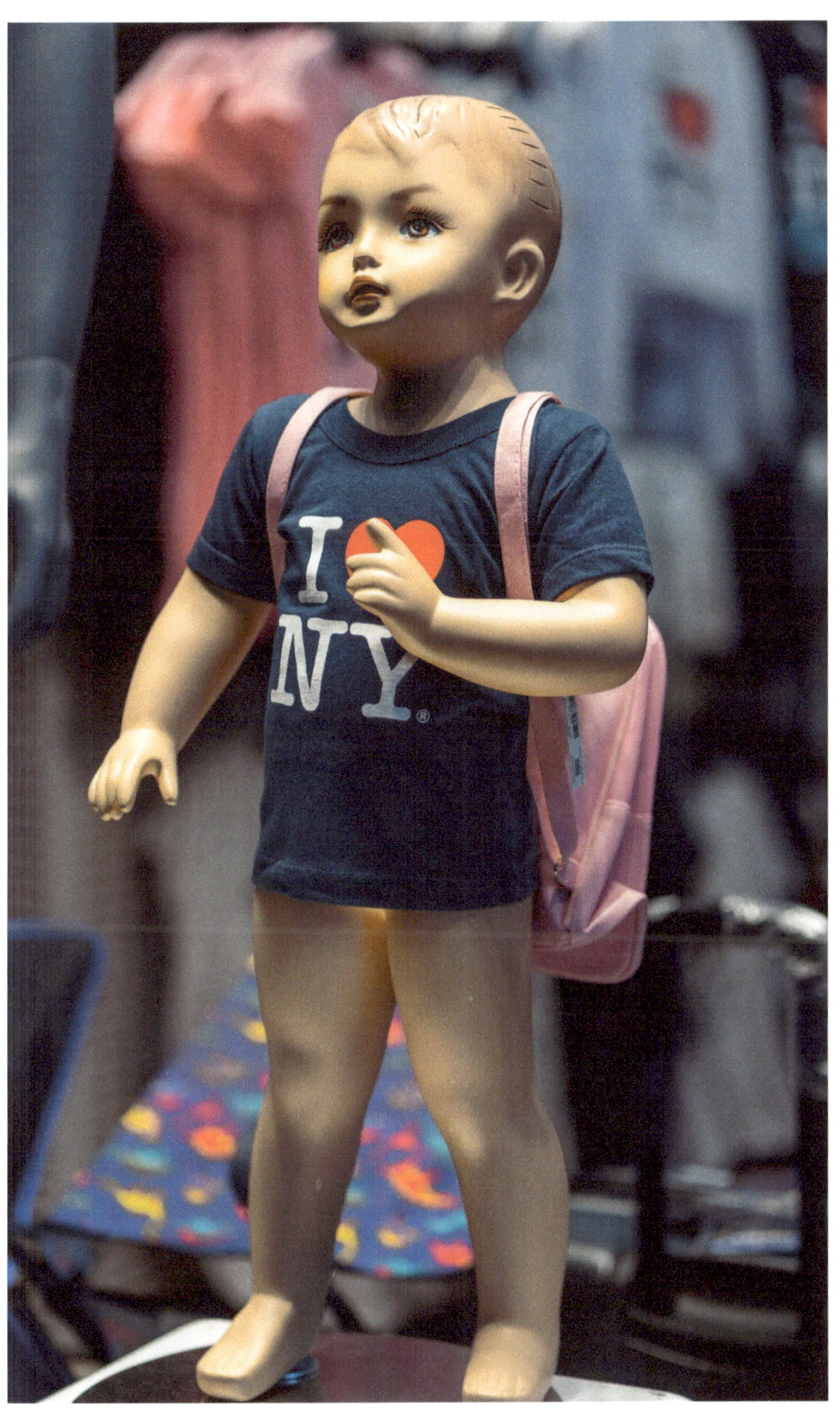

I ❤ NY

CH 8 . ROOMS THAT BREATHE

A museum is the city's hidden breath.
Step inside, and New York's noise quietly withdraws,
leaving only light, shadow,
and a silence that knows how to speak.

Here, people begin to slow.
Some hold their breath before a master's brushstroke;
some loosen their worries in the shadow of a sculpture;
some simply sit—
allowing art to carry what life cannot hold on its own.

These images are about that quiet return:
meeting a long-missed self
within rooms that breathe in stillness.

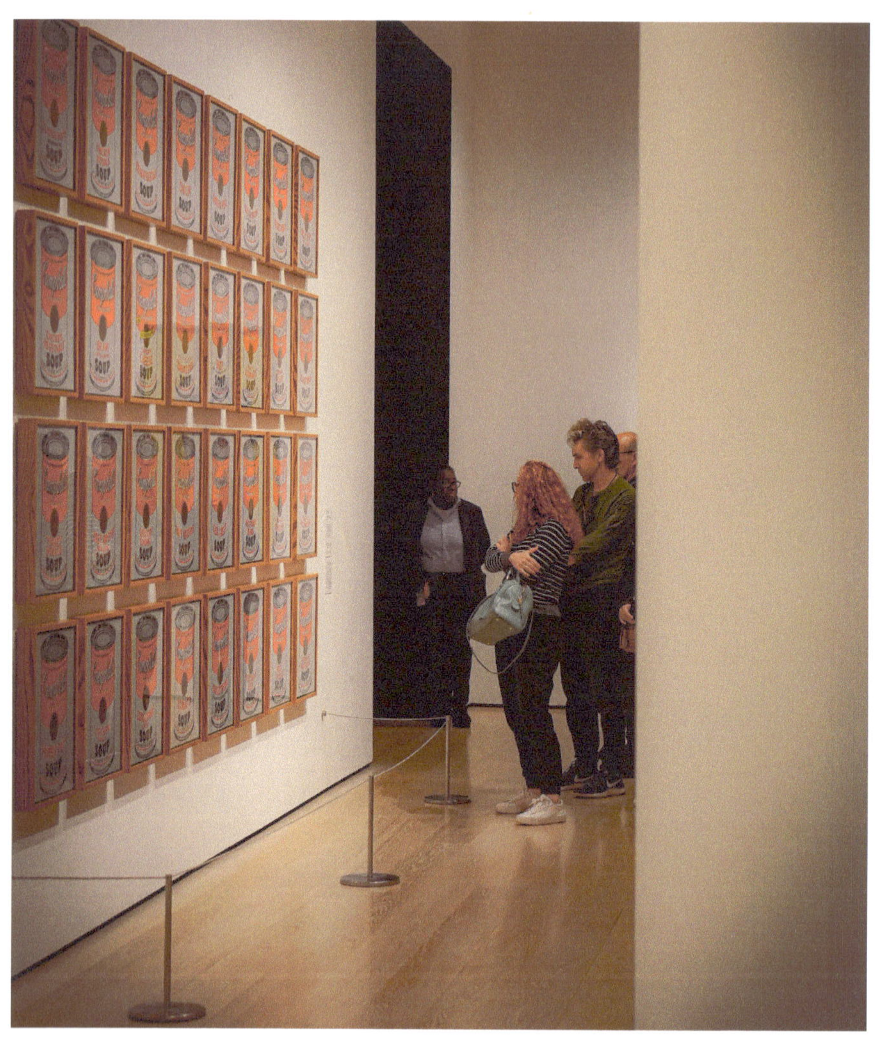

Warhol's repetition becomes a pulse—quietly syncing its breath with those who stop to look.

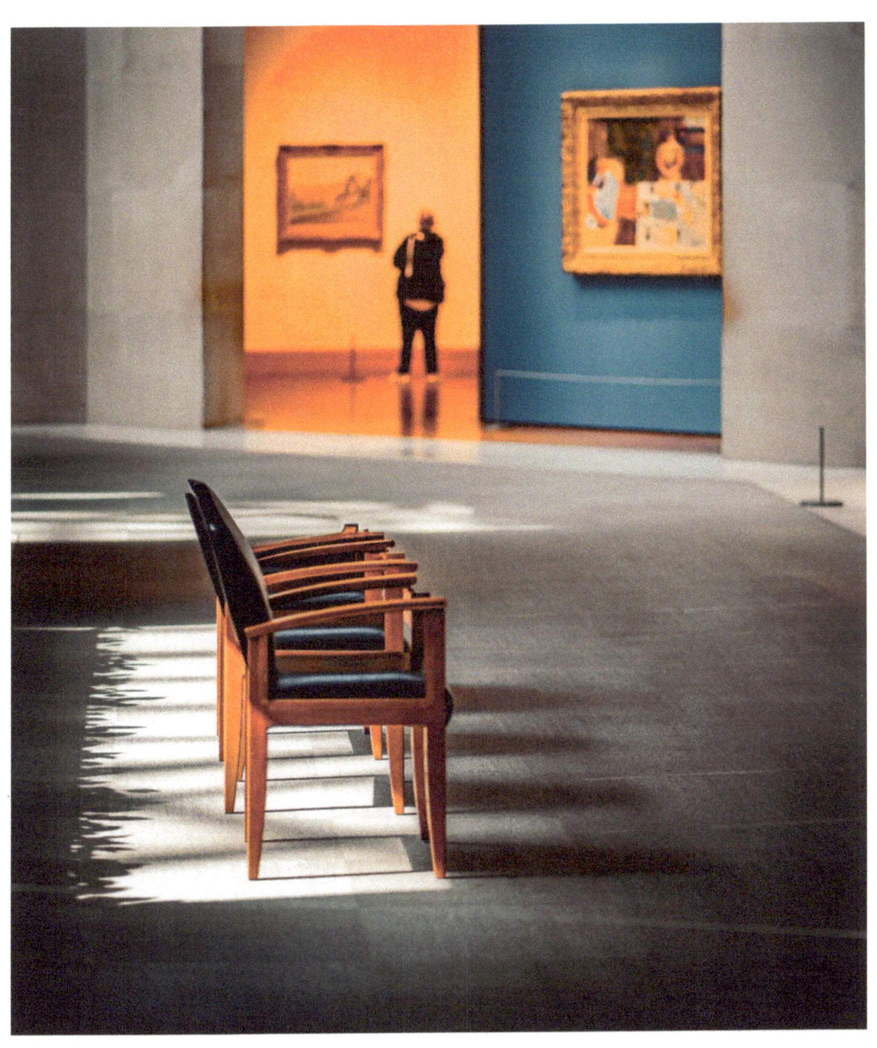

Chairs wait in silence,while the room remembers how to hold a pause.

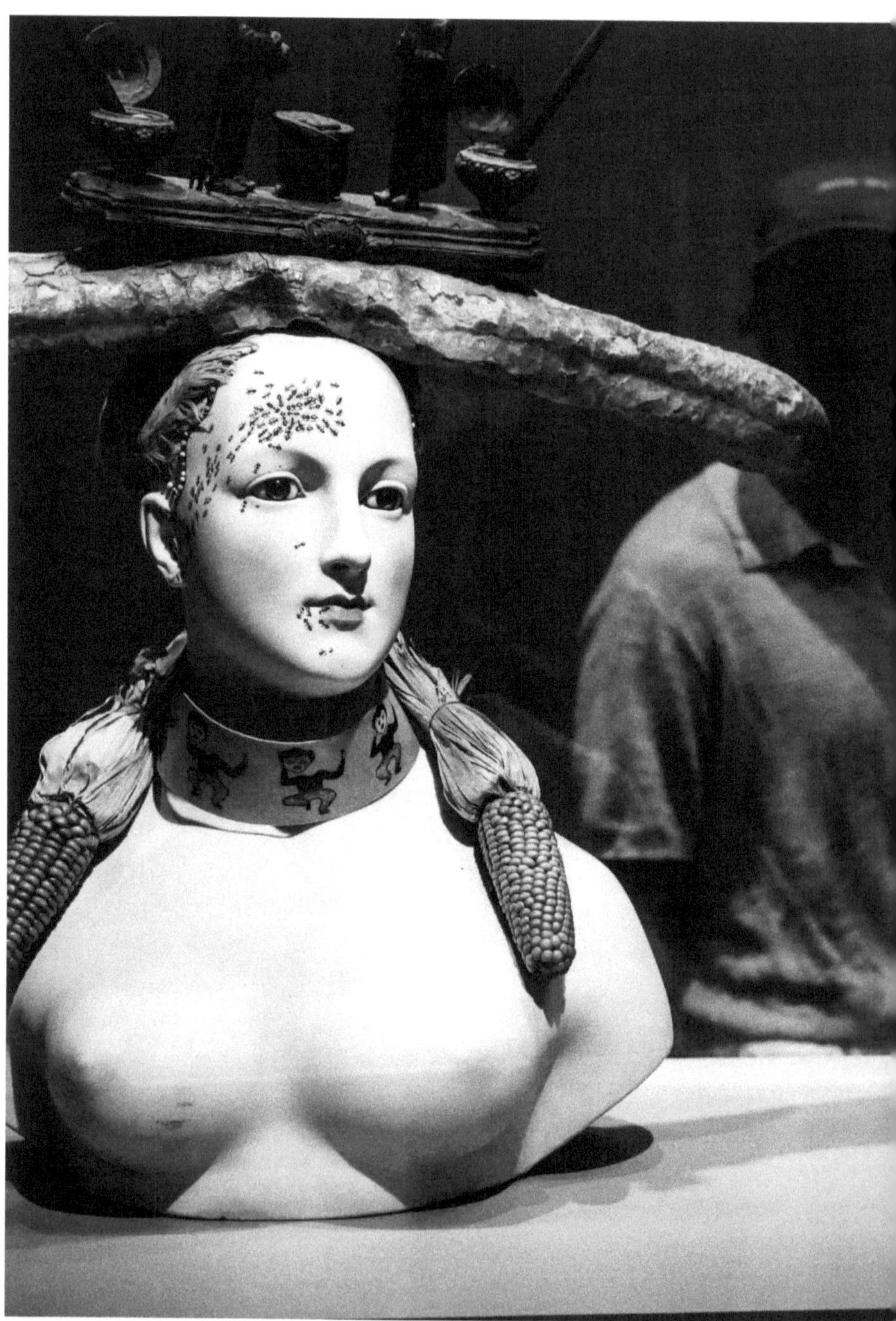

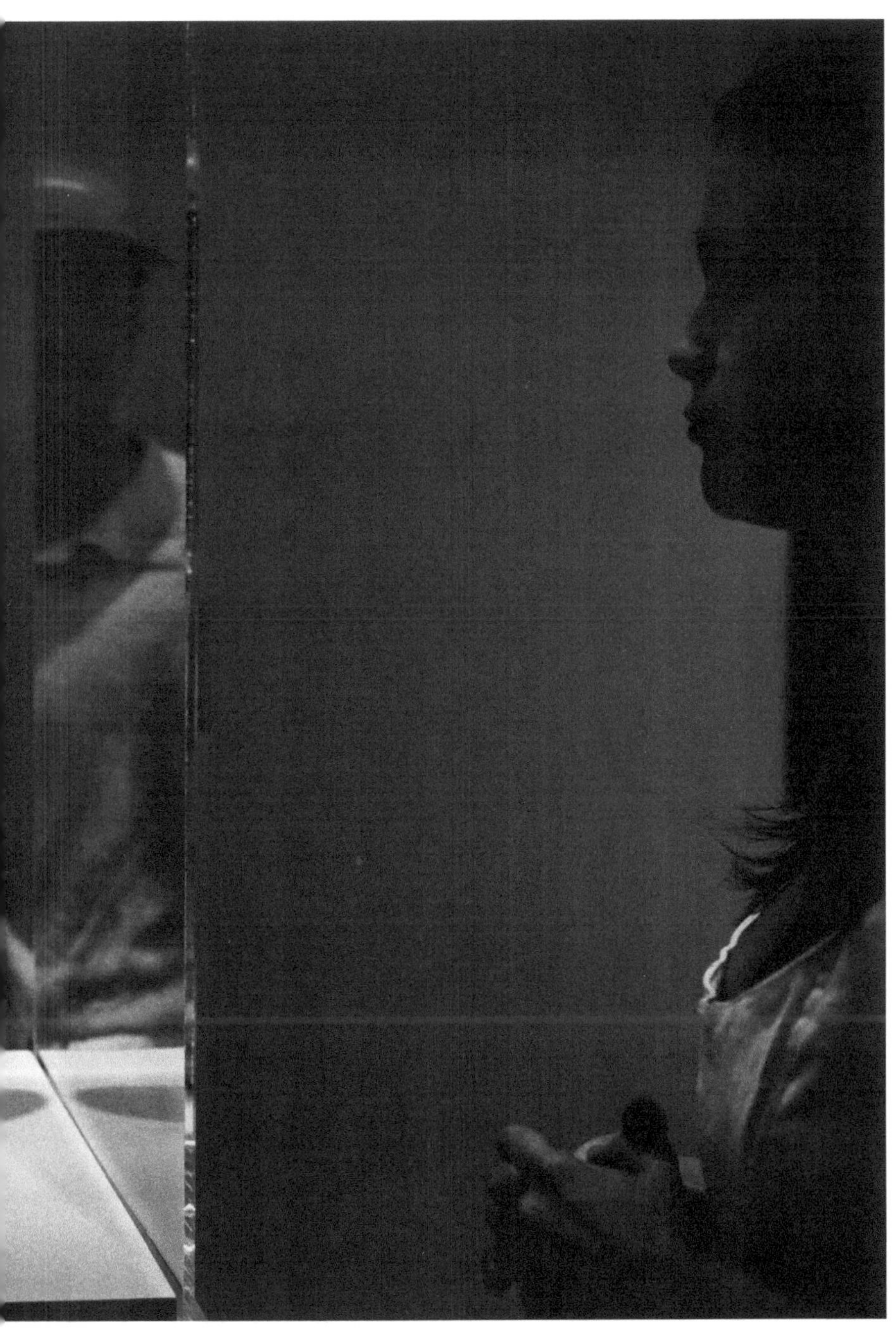

One carved, one reflected, one alive—unsure who is dreaming whom.

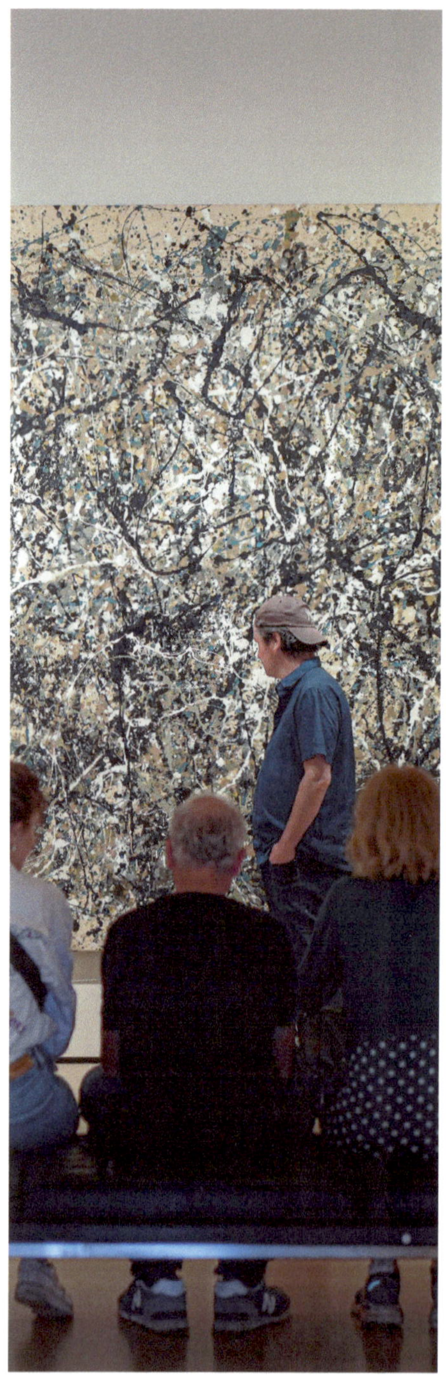

No one has ever finished counting Pollock's lines—and no one ever will.

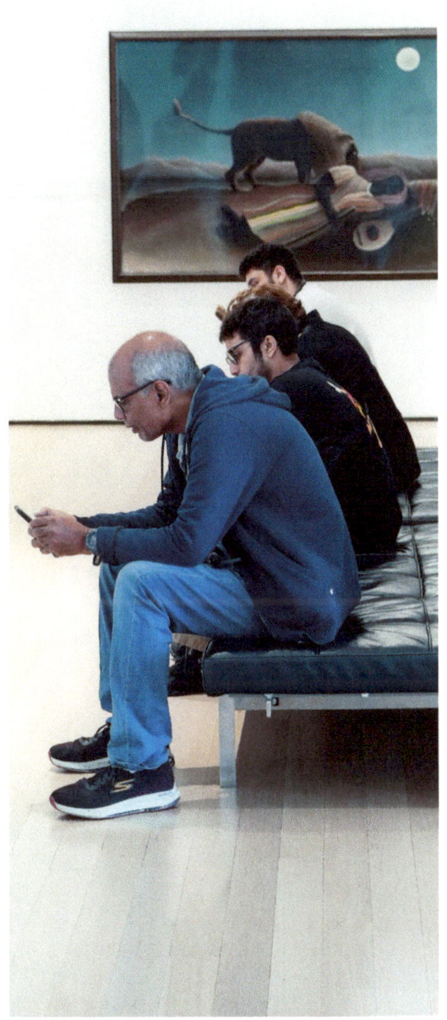

The painting dreams, but the viewers stay
awake by screens brighter than the moon.

We come to see the art, only to find our shadows have taken its place.

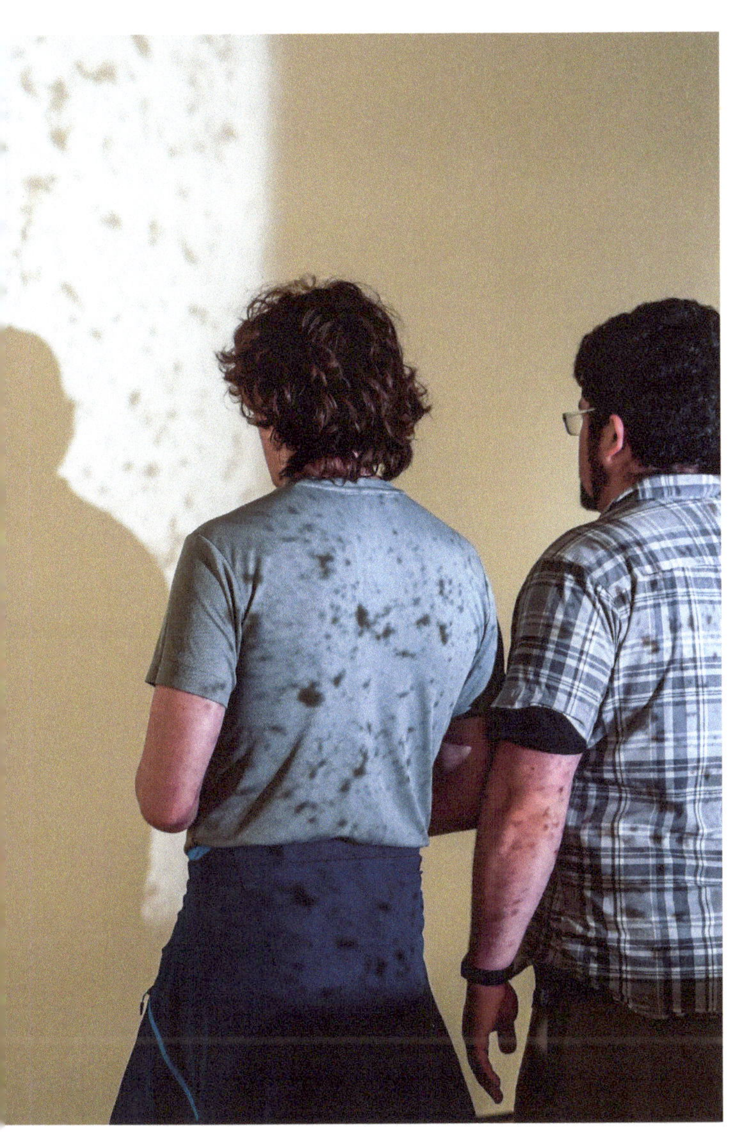

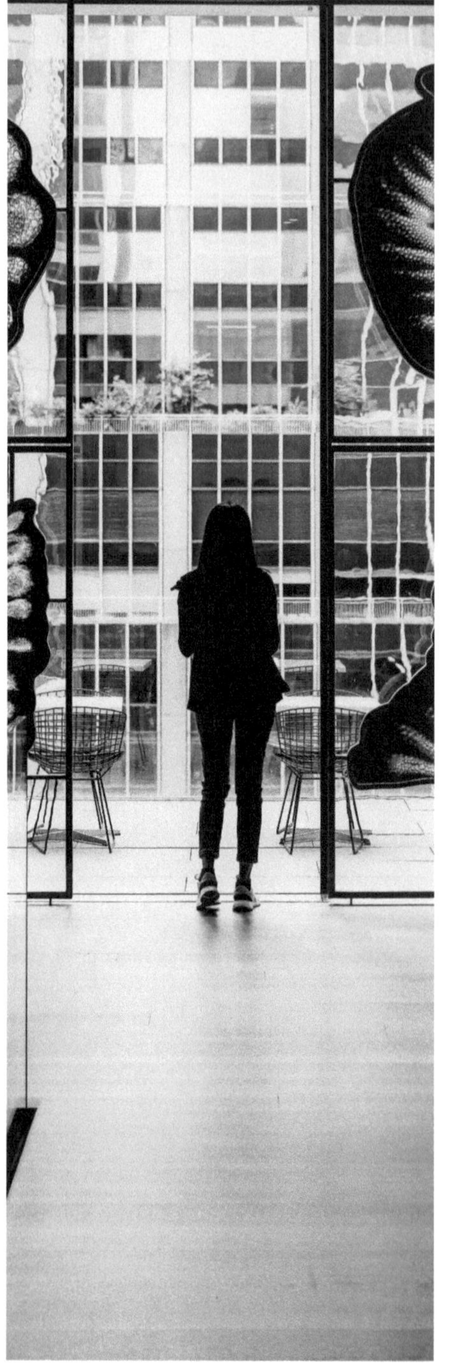

She wakes a forgotten self from the glass.

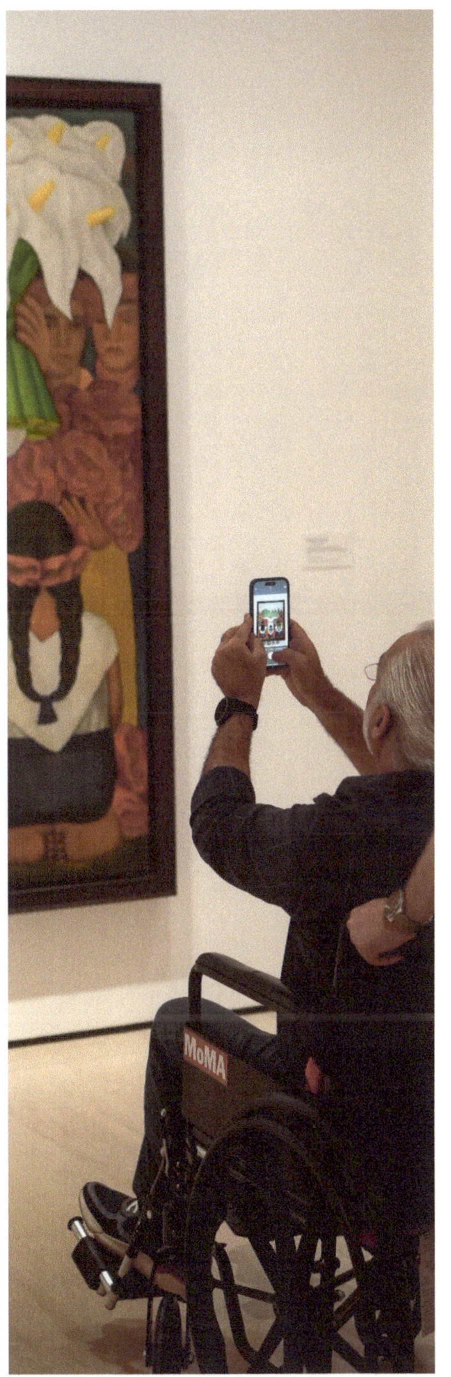

Lift the camera not to remember,
but to feel closer.

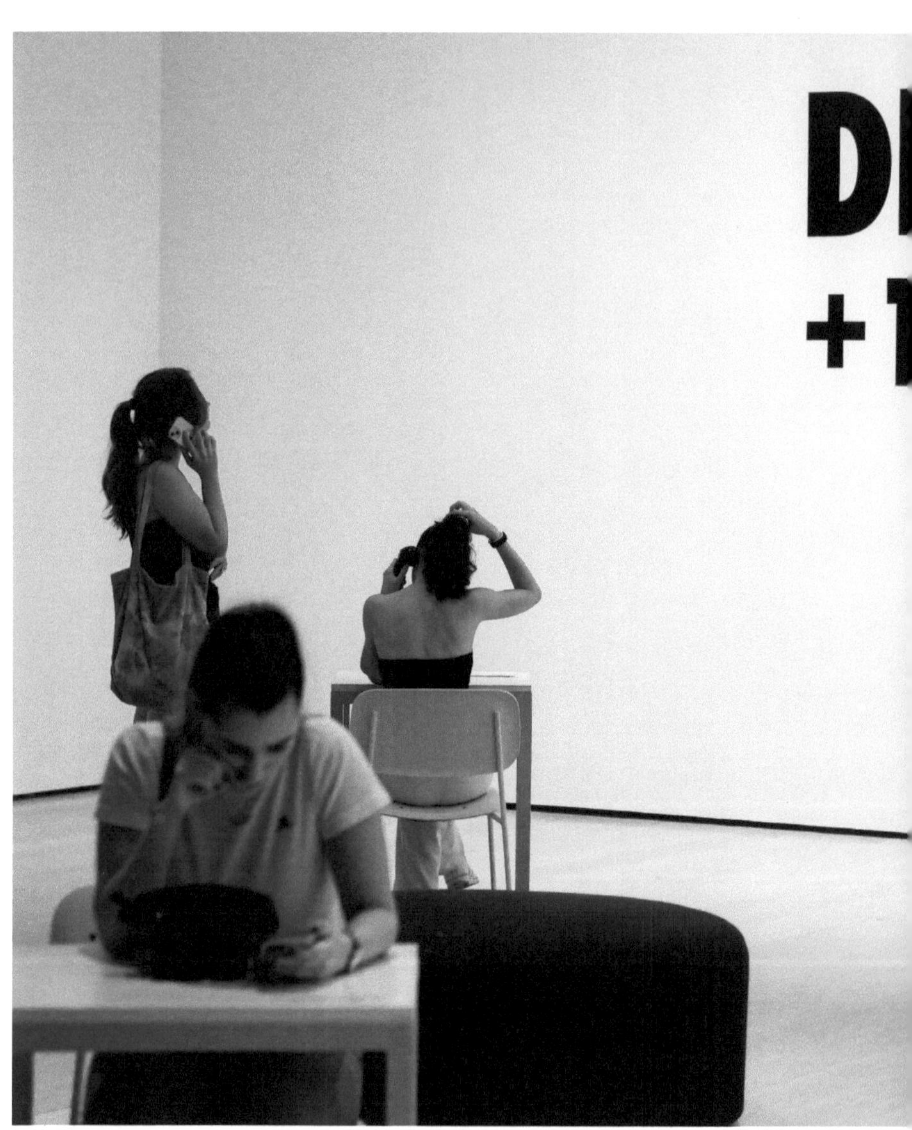
DI
+1

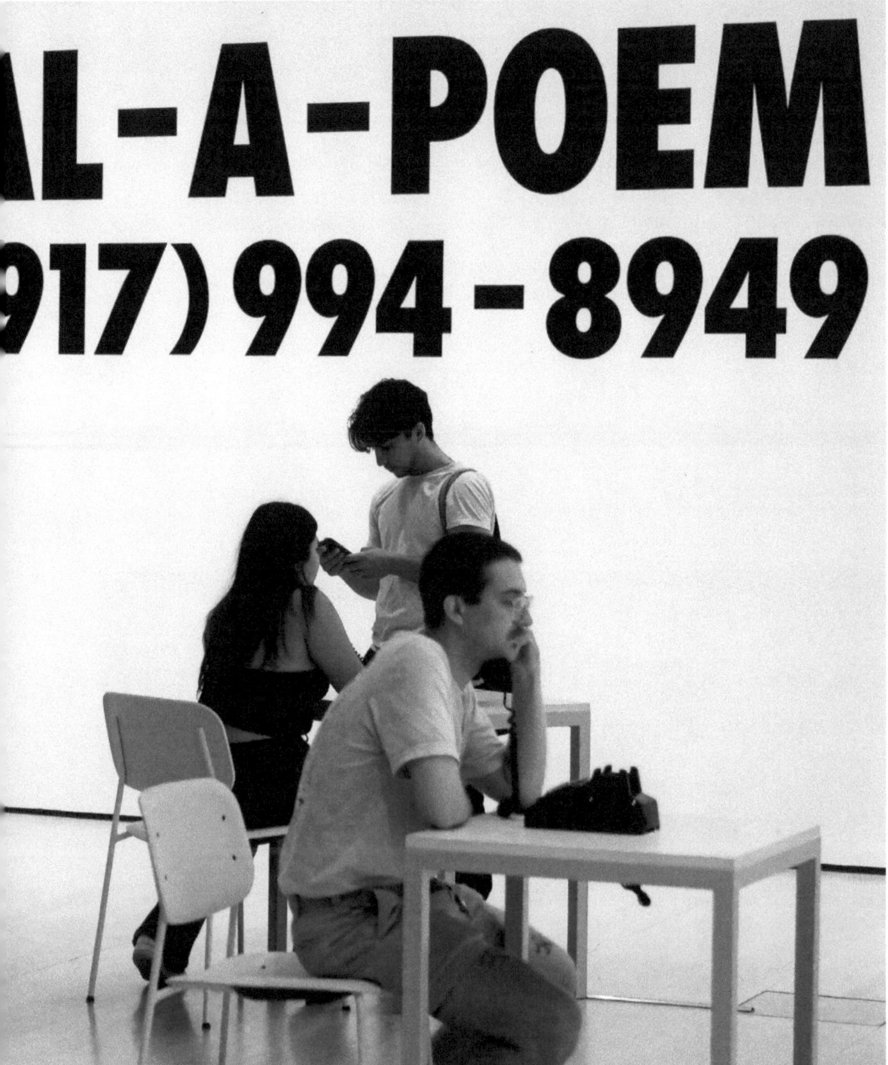

There may be no one on the other end, yet the words always manage to catch us.

She has been looked at for decades. Tonight, she looks back—and finds me.

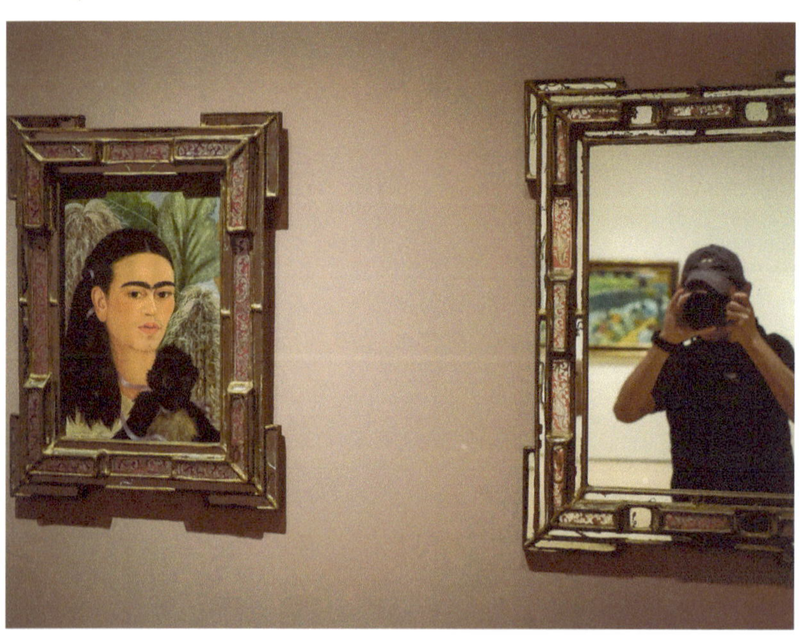

Her gaze slips past the icon,toward the quiet figure framing the moment.

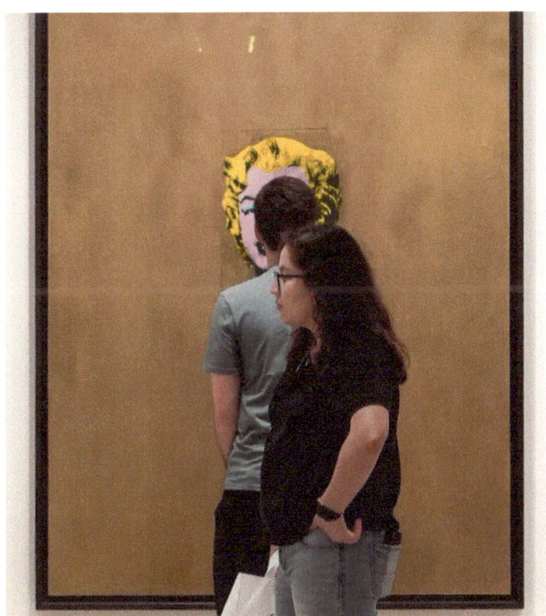

118

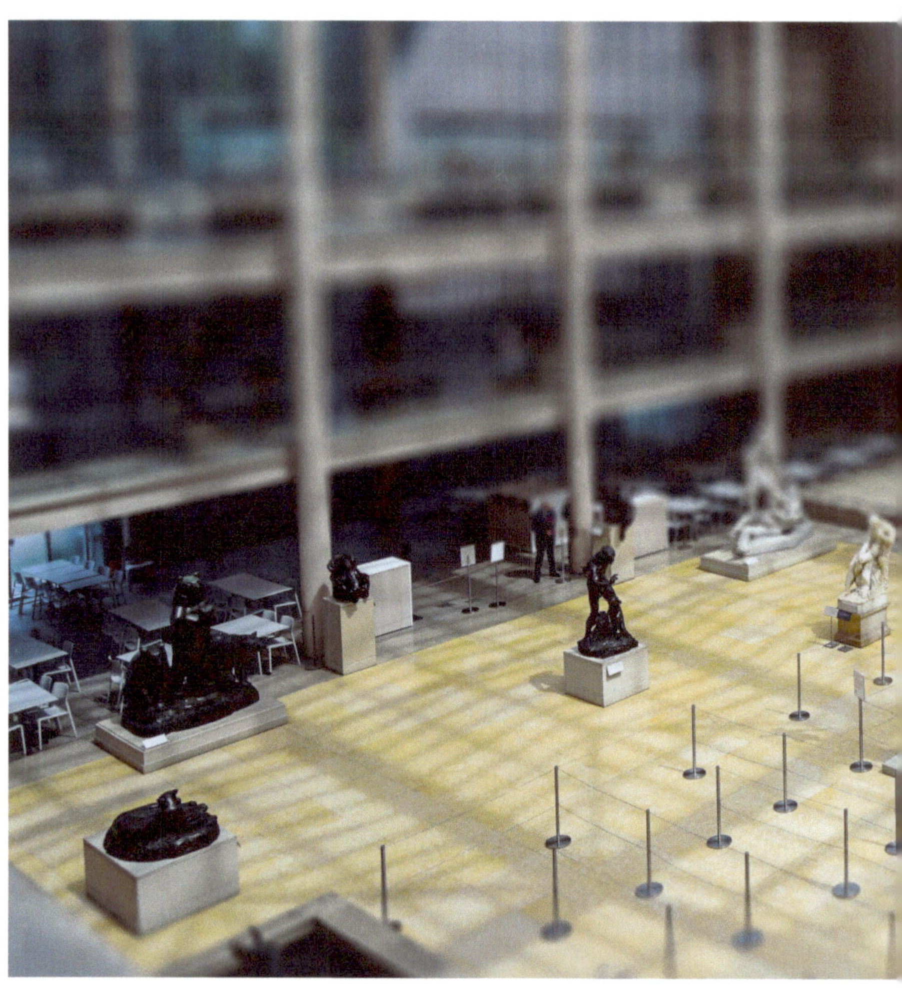

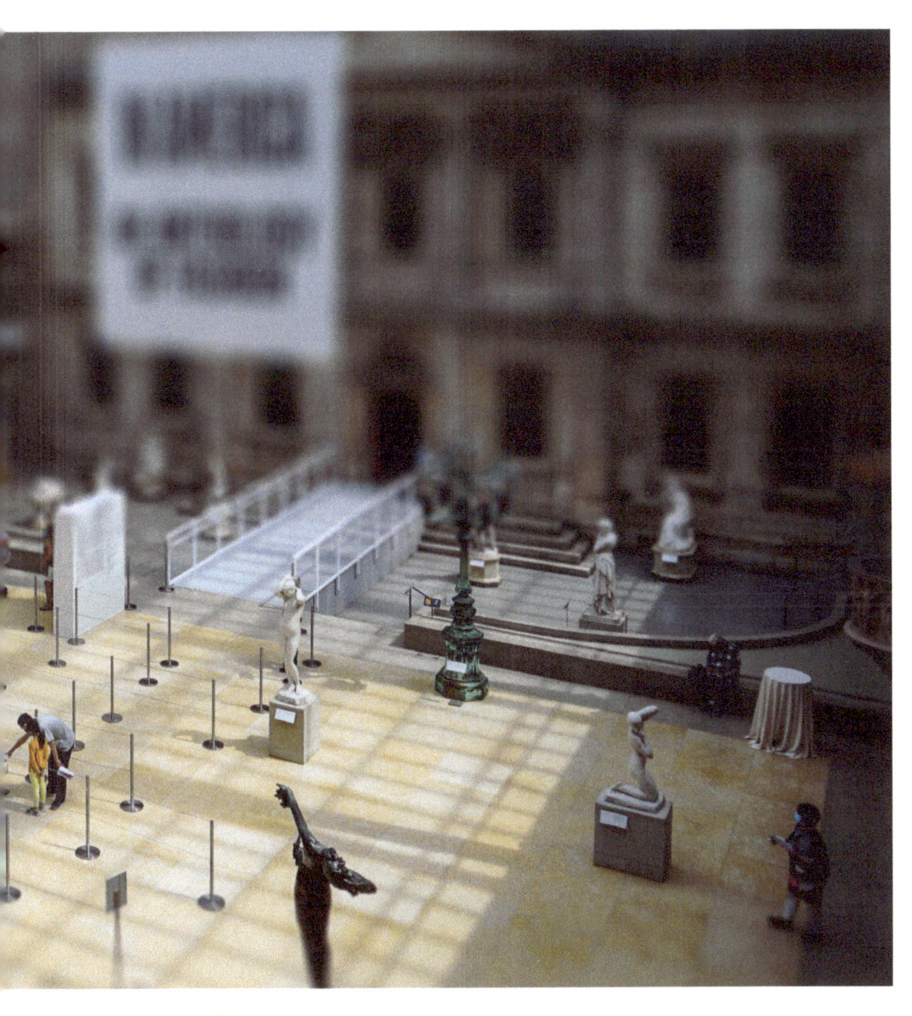

A small world built to explain a larger one we still fail to decode.

CH 9 . BETWEEN HERE AND THERE

Bridges are the city's quietest narrators —
corridors suspended between the known and the unknown,
holding the distance between reality and desire.

We cross them for work, for love, for family,
yet more often, we struggle to cross ourselves —
our hesitations, our memories,
the feelings left unspoken.

A bridge does more than connect two shores.
It links past and future,
the hearts that have yet to meet,
and the unnamed space
between this life and whatever comes after.

Across spans of steel and silence,
New York allows us to walk alone —
without explanation.

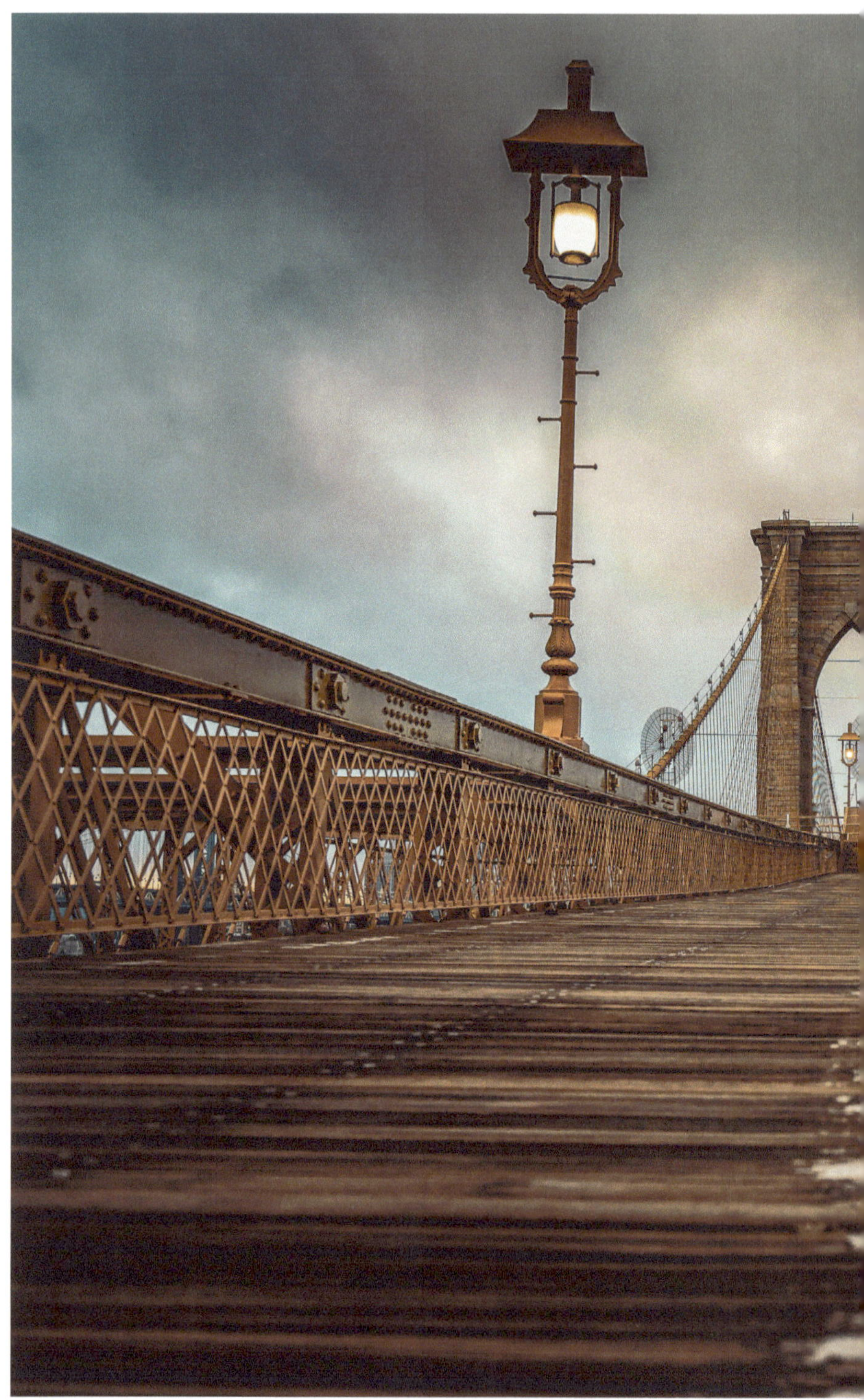

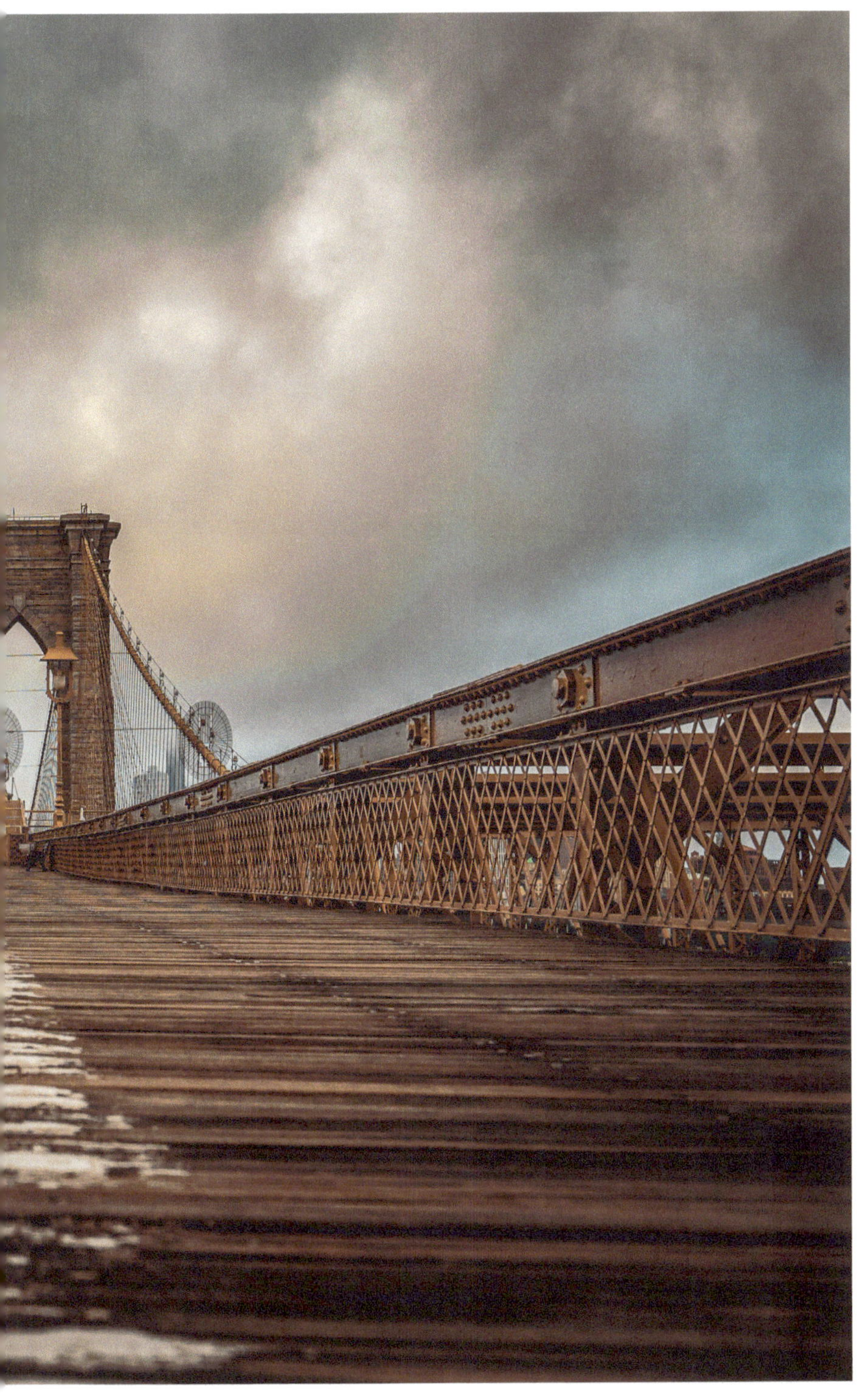

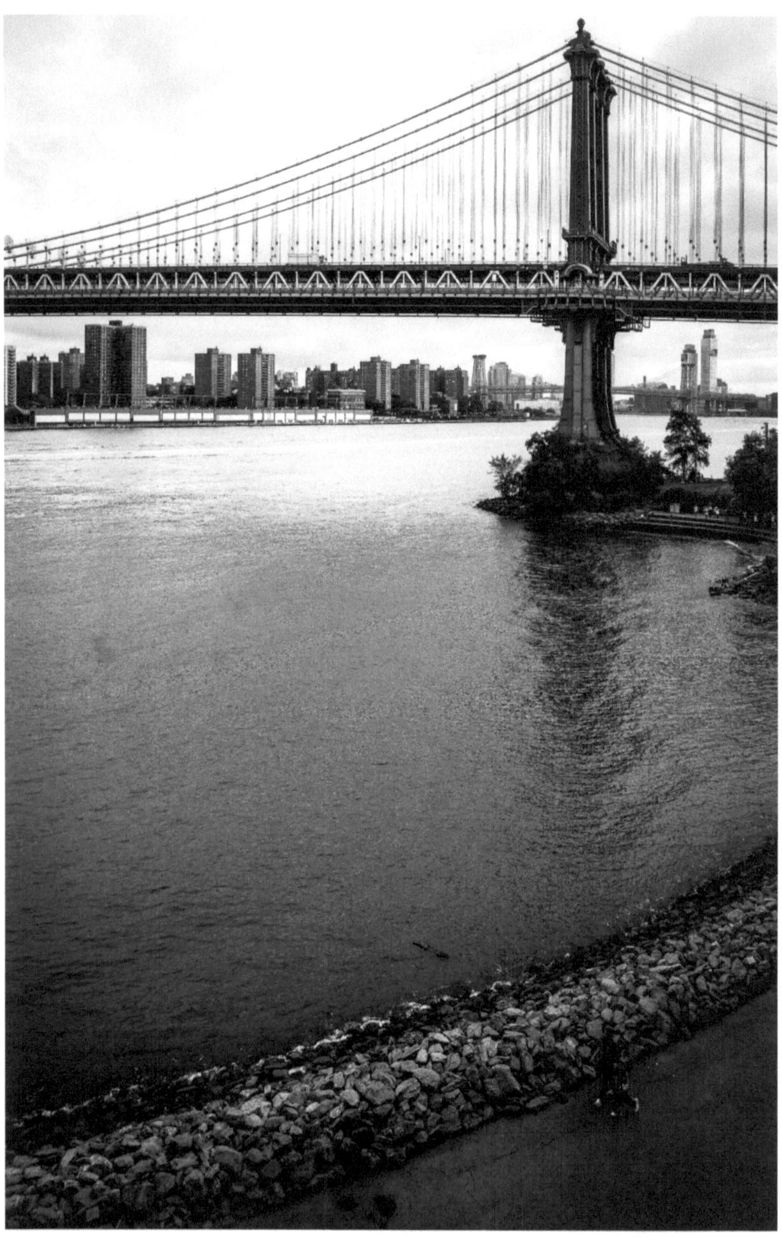

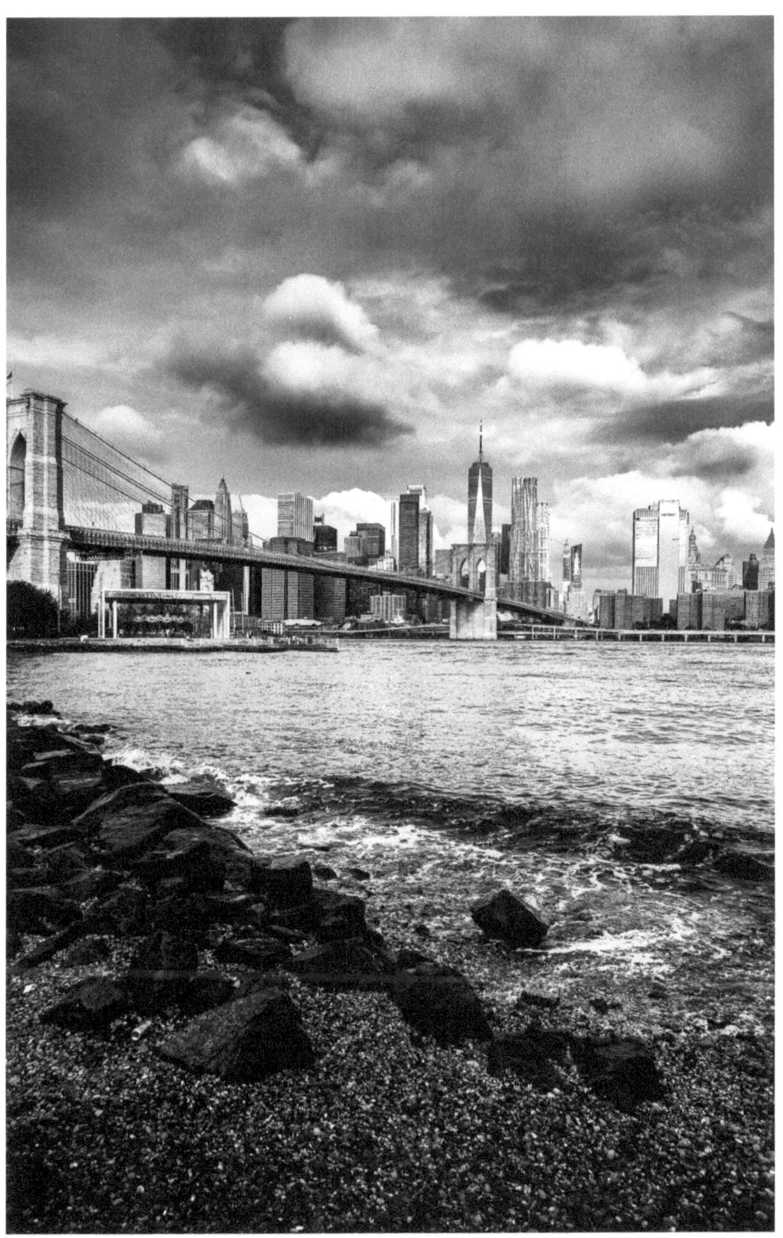

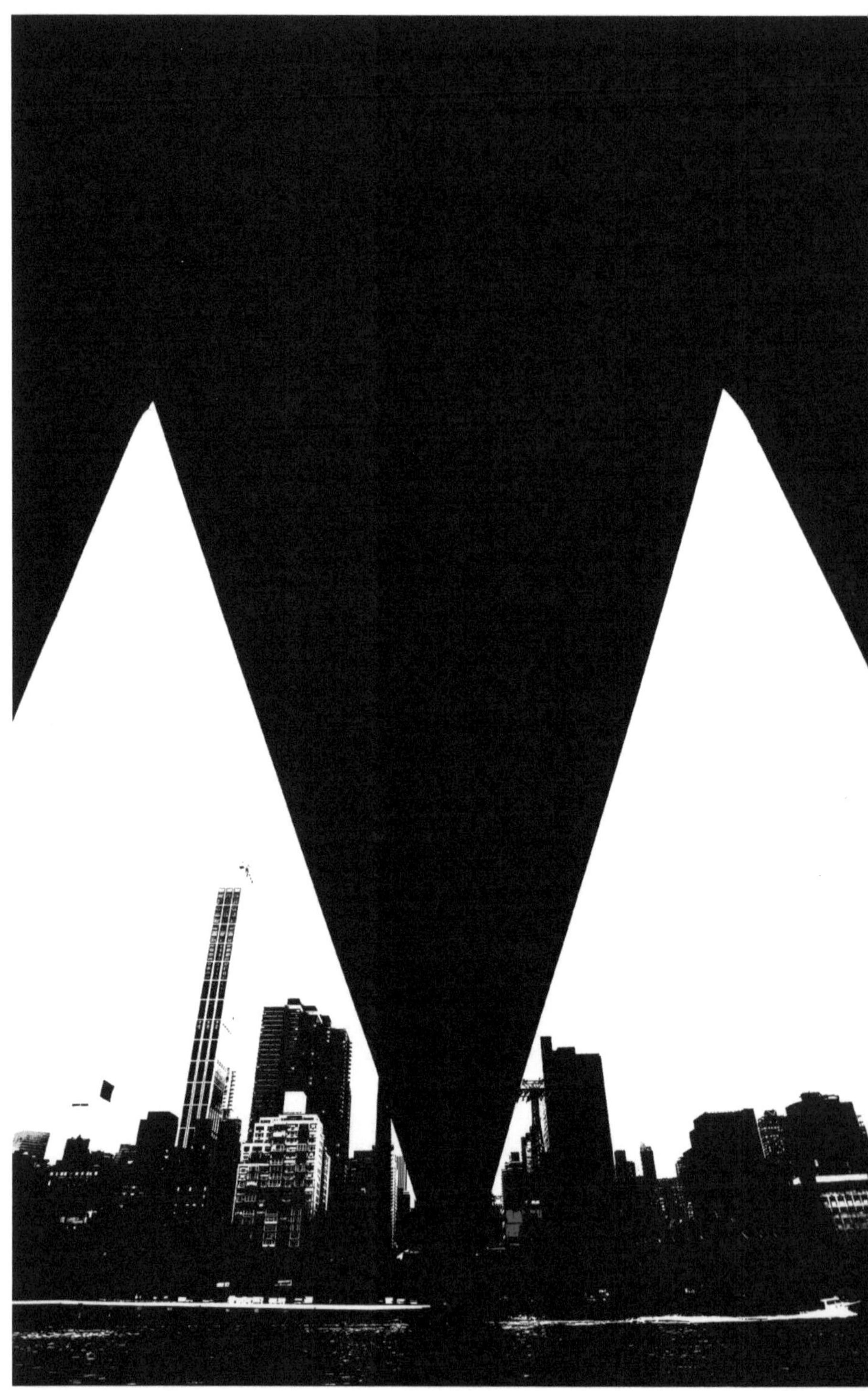

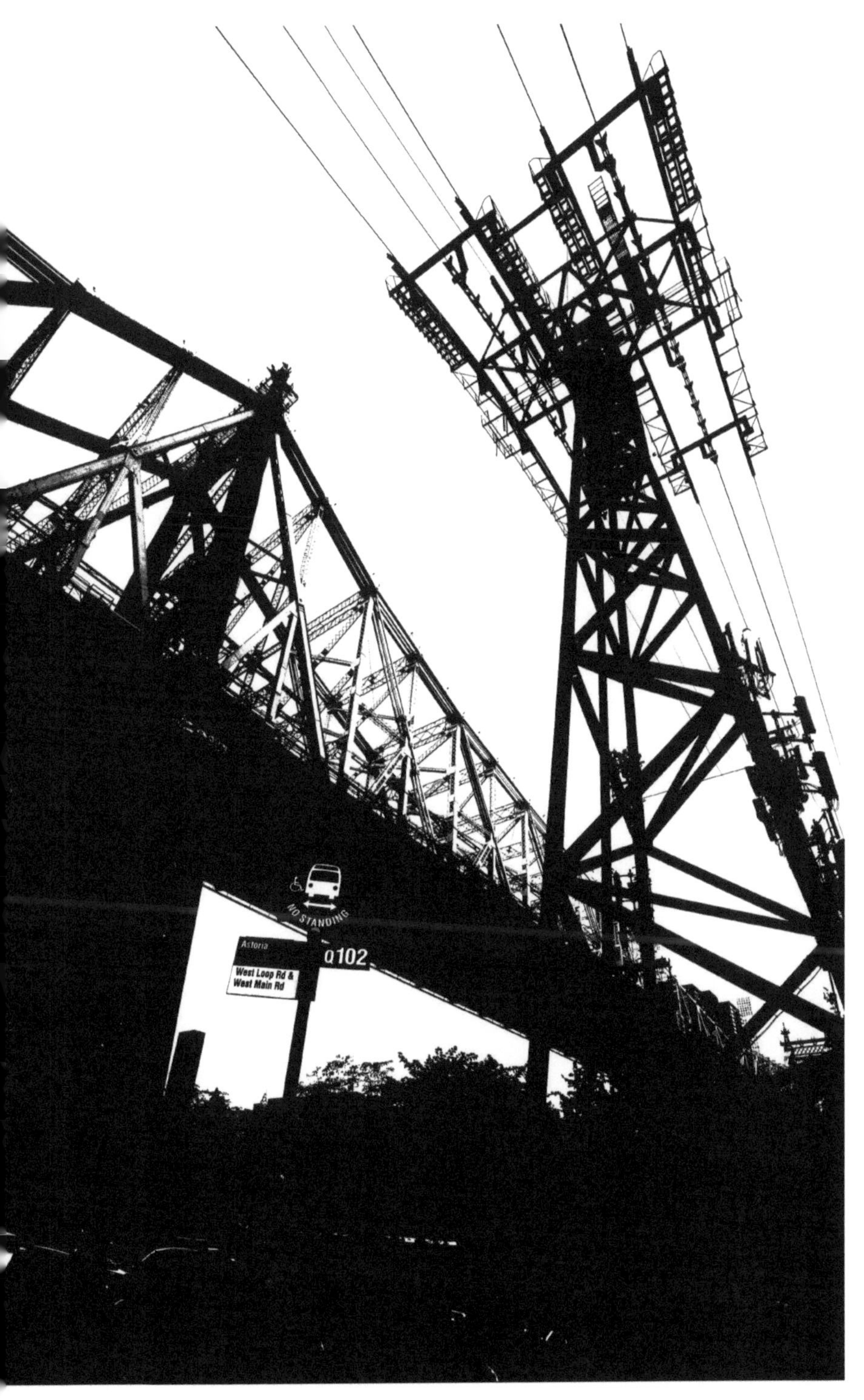
NO STANDING
Astoria
Q102
West Loop Rd &
West Main Rd

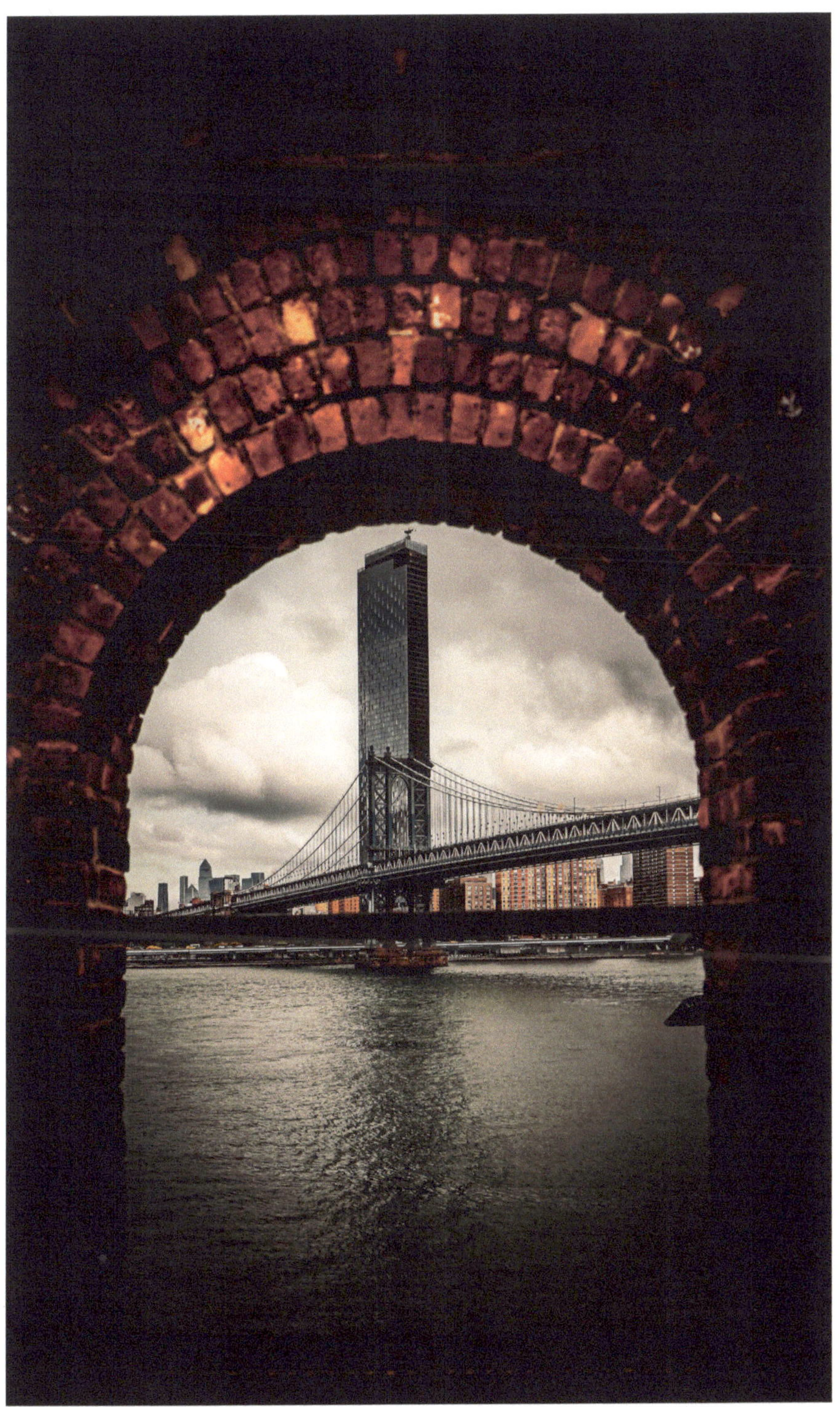

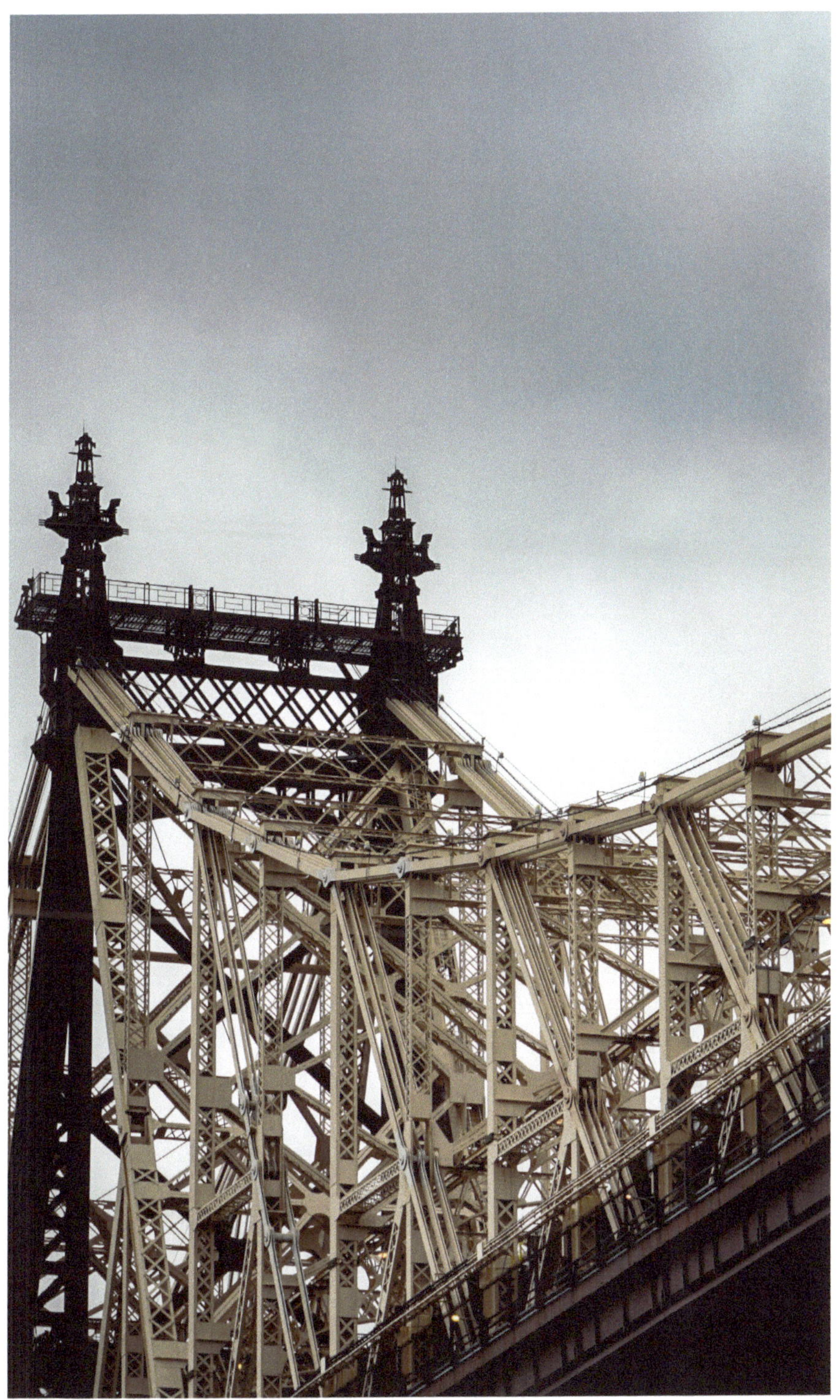

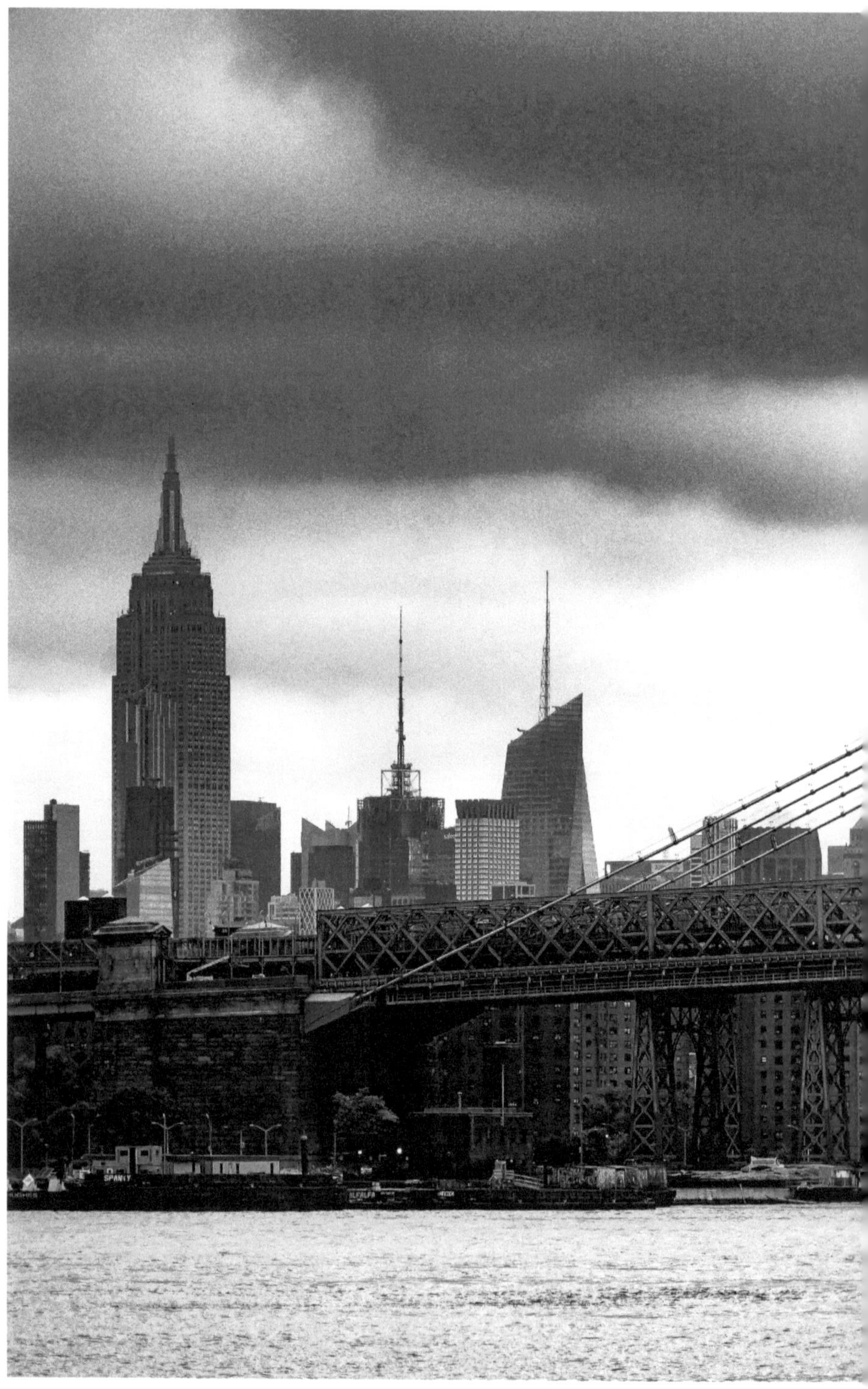

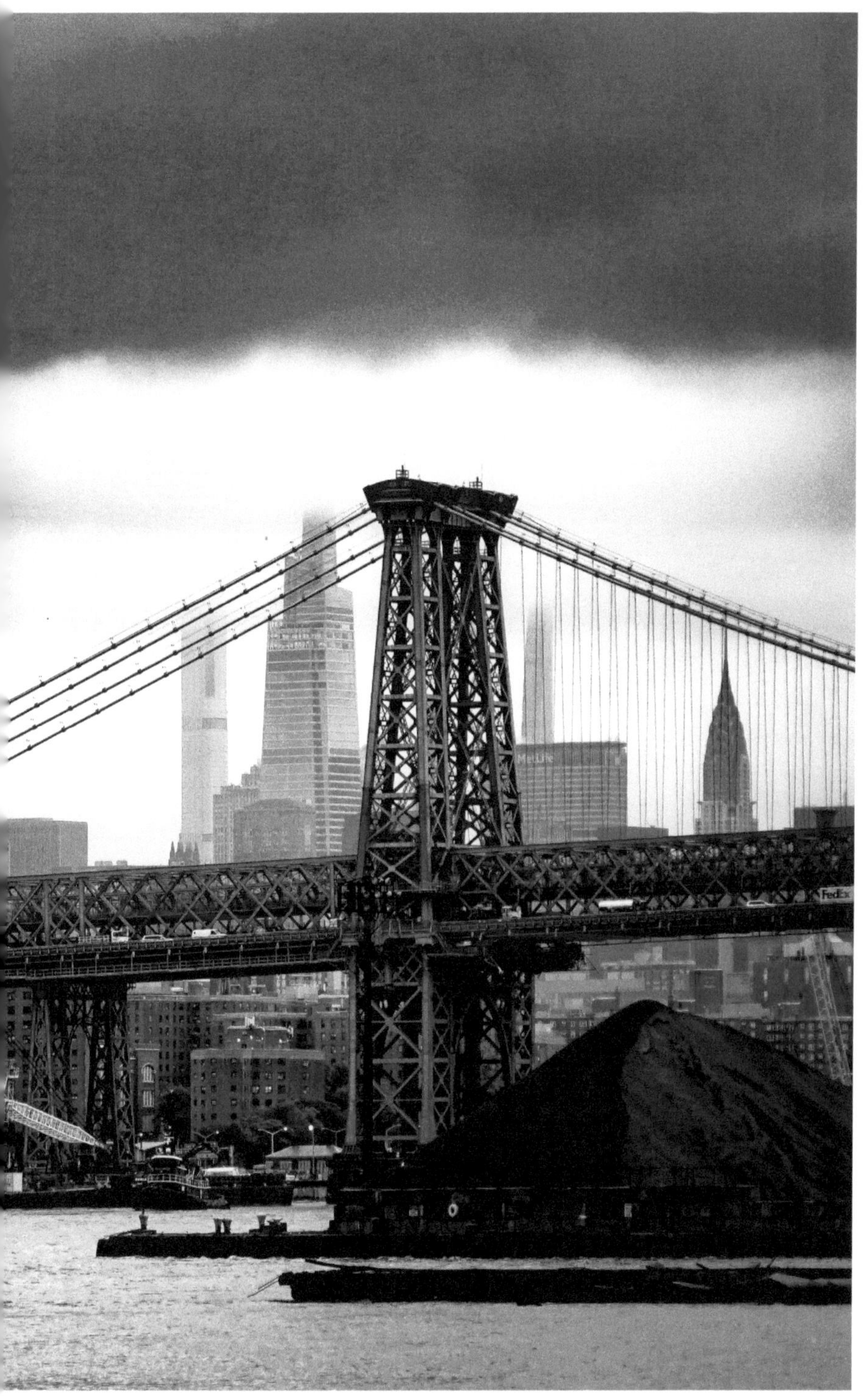

FINAL CH . FOOTPRINTS OF THE HEART

What we remember of a city
is never only its skyline,
but the places where our steps once hesitated,
the moments when a stranger's gaze softened,
the bridges we crossed alone,
and the light that still echoes
long after we've left.

New York has known pain,
has been touched by shadow,
yet it rises again in its own way—
sunlight resting on the Empire State Building
like a vow spoken without words.

The city never truly belonged to us.
We are the ones who left part of ourselves behind:
in the texture of the pavement,
in the reflections of the river,
in the laughter of passing strangers.

May these images become the footprints
that accompany you forward,
quietly, into what comes next.
Even in a city where brilliance and weight coexist,
hope—and connection—
continue to walk beside us.

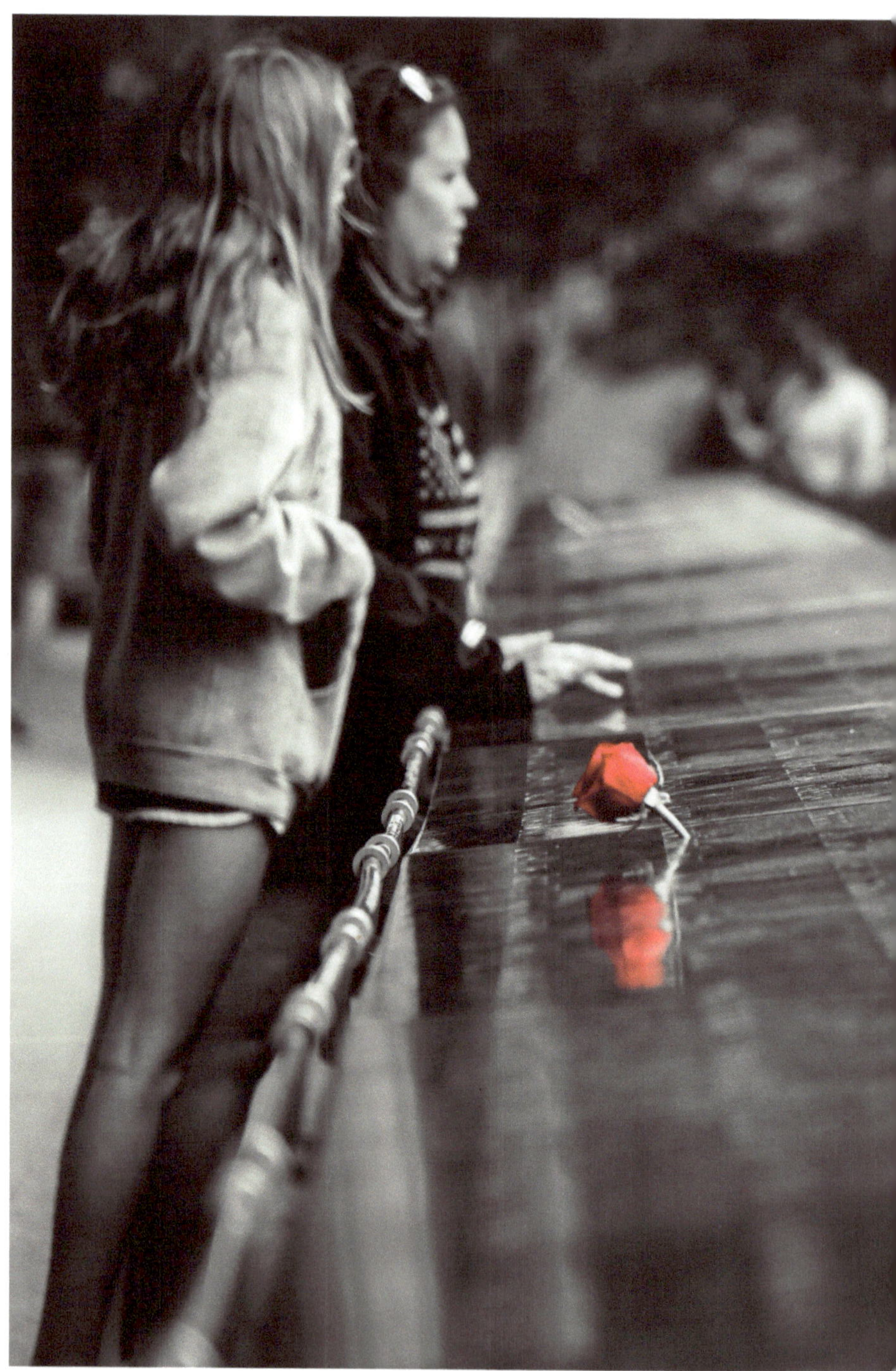

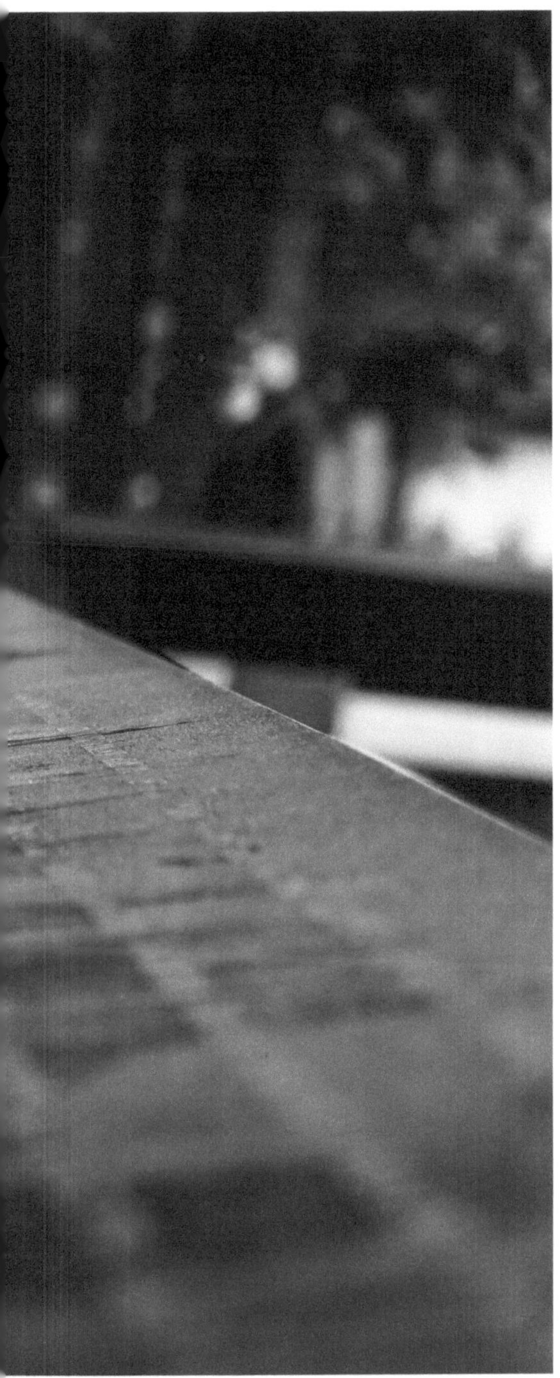

Connection is what survives.